Award-Win
the Dark Side of *The Secret*

The ideas behind Rhonda Byrne's *The Secret* sabotage the human spirit, as one woman learned firsthand . . .the hard way

Her slavish devotion to affirmations and the law of attraction---which refers to the art of demanding spectacular rewards in exchange for little effort---dragged prolific writer Carol Rutter through the bowels of Hell for 17 years. Instead of being rich, thin, and madly in love, she was dead broke and faced a profound medical decline.

Over time, obsessively reciting affirmations meant that her life simply stood still like the calm before a storm. Her life then shattered into a pitiful assortment of tiny fragments as if a tornado had struck.

Rutter does not blame the counterfeit, magical nature of books like Rhonda Byrne's *The Secret* as the spark for her devastating reversal of fortune. Instead, Rutter cites her own gullibility for not recognizing that "If it sounds too good to be true . . ."

In her award-winning book, *Burying the Secret: The Road to Ruin Is Paved with Books about the Law of Attraction*, Rutter offers a fresh and startling analysis of the law of attraction's shadowy side in exhaustive detail and reveals *The Secret's* empty core. "Snake oil at its finest," Rutter writes.

Burying The Secret is inspired by Eastern thought, mysticism, and psychological matters as they relate to spirituality. Laws governing cause and effect, transition, and suffering are significant, as well as key influences like learning lessons, voluntary acts of redemption, sacrifice, and free will.

Citing more than 300 books, Rutter's well-crafted text and savvy perceptions indict *The Secret* for its refusal to acknowledge that unanswered prayers are the norm and for its unfathomable premise: All you have to do is *believe* that dramatic, life-altering changes are possible within 30 days . . . .

A 2008 Eric Hoffer Notable Book Award winner, *Burying the Secret* was acclaimed by *Midwest Book Review* and other reviewers

" . . . provides the reader with an especially articulate, thoughtful, and thought-provoking discussion . . . a seminal work founded on truly impressive research . . . *[Burying the Secret]* is very highly recommended."

Susan Bethany, *Midwest Book Review*

" . . . The 10-page exercise at the back of the book is worth the price alone."

Janet Riehl, http://www.RiehlLife.com

the Burying Secret

The Burying Secret

The Road to Ruin Is Paved with Books About the Law of Attraction

Carol Rutter

Babbling Books
New York

Babbling Books
P.O. Box 4668
New York, NY 10163-4668
http://www.BuryingTheSecret.com

Library of Congress Control Number: 2007908071 (PB)
Rutter, Carol.
Burying the secret: the road to ruin is paved with
books about the law of attraction by Carol Rutter.
Index.
Bibliography.
1. Self-help 2. Spiritual.
ISBN 978-0-9798609-0-4 (PB)
ISBN 978-0-9798609-1-1 (Lrg. Print)

First Babbling Books edition January 1, 2008
Front cover artwork: Rani Akoub
Page layout and cover design: Adina Cucicov
Manufactured in the United States of America
Please visit http://www.BuryingTheSecret.com
for detailed contact information or email
Media at BuryingTheSecret.com.

This book is dedicated to everyone whose dreams and aspirations have been postponed indefinitely by life's inevitable detours.

Contents

Acknowledgements

Editorial

I extend my gratitude to **Mary Akashah** who is such a gifted editor that she transformed raw, flawed material into a polished and professional manuscript. Mary's attunement to nearly imperceptible subtleties astonished me on a daily basis.

Thanks to **René Howard,** who brilliantly edited an early incarnation of this book.

I also deeply appreciate all the wisdom and consummate writing advice that was so freely given to me by the late **Lisa Black Burn.**

Front Cover Artwork

Rani Akoub's artwork far exceeded my expectations because he enhanced my original concept with his stunning, surreal vision. Rani can be contacted at kekke84 at hotmail.com.

Page Layout and Cover Design

Adina Cucicov worked very hard within a tight schedule to satisfy my countless requests for revisions. Her skills, flexibility, and professional attitude made her a pleasure to work with. Adina can be reached by email at maricuci73 at yahoo.it.

Creative Muses

The work of **Peter Tolan** and **Denis Leary** consistently fired up my creative embers, which were nearly extinguished at times. Their partnership served as a constant reminder to boldly take chances, to never settle for mediocrity, and to *always* set the bar higher.

Inspiration for Content

I discuss authors **Alice Miller, Caroline Myss, Susanne Short**, and **Sandra Thomson** in such favorable terms that it might lead the reader to incorrectly assume I have a personal connection to them. I do not know these people, or anyone associated with them, yet I am very grateful I found their respective writings when I did.

Other prescient authors also influenced my spiritual development and informed this book. These individuals produced works of such high quality and with so many startling insights, that I would be remiss if I failed to cite their contributions to metaphysical writings as a whole.

In particular, I acknowledge the works of **Jeremiah Abrams, Robert Bly, John Bradshaw, Gina Cerminara, Clarissa Pinkola Estes, Marilyn Ferguson, Thaddeus Golas, Pamela Rae Heath, Robert A. Johnson, Carl J. Jung, John Klimo, Richard Linklater, Ralph Metzner, Deng Ming-Dao, Raymond Moody, Melvin Morse, Christiane Northrup, Sogyal Rinpoche, Jane Roberts, Dorothee Soelle, Thomas Szasz, Robert Thurman, Chogyam Trungpa, Evelyn Underhill, Alan Watts, Marianne Williamson, Paramahansa Yogananda, Gary Zukav,** and **Connie Zweig.**

Personal Encouragement

I also thank **Scott Curtis, Harald Kaltz, Anthony Mills, Caroline Nabozniak, Robert Prost, Lynne Zelms,** and **Zelmo Zelms** for their unconditional love and support, which spanned many long years.

Finally, I thank **Lee Rhinehart Hall, Tim Hall, Lily Hall,** and **Rory Hall** for their love, encouragement, and unwavering belief in me and this project when few others saw the point.

the Burying Secret

Introduction

Burying the Secret reflects my feverish devotion to the "law of attraction" in the late 1980s when I believed that dream fulfillment was always just around the corner. Drunk with denial, I staggered into Hell instead. Back then, I believed all the writers who promised that the law of attraction converts our desires into concrete outcomes through positive-thinking strategies such as visualizations and affirmations.

Over time, rattling off affirmations every day meant that my life simply stood still, shortly before it shattered into a pitiful assortment of tiny fragments. I spent a lot of time rummaging around for usable shards like a homeowner searching for salvageable items after a tornado leveled her house.

Rhonda Byrne's *The Secret*

Editor Rhonda Byrne and *The Secret's* 24 contributors would have us believe that the law of attraction supersedes all other Universal laws, because no other forces governing our lives are mentioned in the book, let alone their interrelationships and potential pecking order. Furthermore, *The Secret* fails to acknowledge that *unanswered* prayers and long-postponed outcomes represent the norm for life-altering changes.

Rather than disputing the existence of the law of attraction, *Burying The Secret* discusses *The Secret's* numerous restrictions and oversights. However, the bulk of *Burying The Secret* examines other Universal laws and spiritual issues inextricably linked to the law of attraction.

Burying The Secret favors a nondenominational approach, yet seasoned metaphysical readers will likely recognize the book's Eastern and mystical influences.

Part 1

The Law of Attraction

The complete expression of everything of which we are capable—the whole psychological zoo living within us, as well as the embryonic beginnings of artist, statesman, or saint—[entails] chaos, not character.

Evelyn Underhill
The Spiritual Life

Chapter 1

Confessions of a New Age Junkie

Hello, my name is Carol and I am a New Age junkie. My drug of choice is affirmations.

Hi, Carol.

I cannot recall a hand basket when I went to Hell in the early 1990s as a result of following the law of attraction to the letter. I just knew that I had never sunk so low. I also failed to forecast that the worst was yet to come. Things got so bad that all concrete attempts to reverse my unstoppable slide into deep poverty—and the resulting social alienation—were completely useless. I became an outcast because everyone viewed me as a loser with a capital L, except for longstanding close friends.

I experienced unprecedented levels of frustration as I hit one brick wall after another. At times, I felt that only a fine, fragile line kept me from crossing over into full-fledged madness. Nevertheless, short-lived periods of near-insanity and/or depression did take over from time to time. Desperation would render me hopeless and helpless until such time as I would mysteriously revive and begin to struggle once again. Occasionally, the recovery was so feeble that I planned my suicide. Once, I even composed multiple goodbye letters. Their tone reflected more misery and bewilderment than bitterness.

Confidantes kept telling me that the law of attraction was doing me in, though the buzz words in those days were more typically "transformation," "healing," and "prosperity thinking." Ten years passed before I could adapt to my unprecedented subsistence-level existence, but this whole sorry period spanned 17 years altogether.

Hindsight Is the Greatest Teacher

I eventually learned that prayers, affirmations, and visualizations are all well and good in moderation, as long as they refer to trivial matters such as productive bargain hunting or getting great tickets to a popular concert. I ultimately understood that climbing up the ladder to address more life-altering issues represents another matter entirely: Utilizing real-world resources to solve life's problems provides the only workable approach. A dash of optimism fuels these efforts, but positive thinking—without concrete strategies—either produces no results or propels us into unwanted situations, no matter how fiercely we resist them.

I now understand that many immovable obstacles far outweighed viable solutions in this dark period. I also can see that my frustrations and failures produced important insights; I could not move on until vital life lessons had been incorporated into my psyche. Chief among these was purging prosperity thinking because it had figuratively and literally bankrupted me. Once I gave up affirmations and took personal responsibility, my life improved. Accepting reality—warts and all—was another key feature of my recovery.

The Transformation Blues

During this period, I would find myself rattled and skittish for several months after a trying situation ended. In one case, it took the form of panic when I heard a knock at the door or the phone ringing. The erratic people associated with my most recent horror had no way of knowing where I had moved, but for a few seconds I believed it was one of them visiting or dialing, until I got a grip. Despite all of this, my walk over the embers in Hell yielded some rewards as these two examples illustrate:

First, I used to be a raging bull with a combustible temperament, breathing fire several times a day over nothing. I now have a very long fuse and find that the repertoire of things eliciting anger has all but disappeared.

Second, my dangerously impulsive nature has given way to extraordinary patience.

In retrospect, I realize that my life *had* to stop dead in its tracks to get my attention, so that I could learn a multitude of lessons. I could not have addressed these challenges in a meaningful fashion without the relentless adversities I faced for a very long time. I emerged from the chaos created by my affirmation addiction to enjoy a far more stable life. That might not sound like much, but I am grateful because I could only dream of stability for a very long time.

Before the Tides Turned

Oddly enough, stability and security had anchored my life until I opened up that New Age can of worms. In the time before my life disintegrated, I was living well in Montreal. I had a good job, a fabulous apartment, and a $7,000 annual budget for clothes and my beloved shoe collection. I worked out at least six hours every week and was in perfect health, as long as I did not count my lifelong battle with weight control. Despite the obesity, I looked presentable and enjoyed a rich social life.

During this period, I was at the tail end of work on a film degree and had already accumulated impressive writing credits. I had traveled to New York and Los Angeles several times to cover film festivals and interview Hollywood notables. Prestigious magazines had published these articles. In addition, an academic conference had accepted an independent study I did on advances in film technology and it was later published by a film journal. Some of my professors were quite stunned by this because most of these events took place while I was still a freshman.

Rumblings before the Storm

Shortly before graduating in 1988, I began to experience an uncomfortable restlessness. I desperately wanted a career change and had spent 10 long years working towards my degree on a part-time basis while employed full time as a well-compensated accountant, though I did not have a CPA degree. However, I had no idea how I would find rewarding film work in Canada. Local pickings were slim to none and staying in Montreal meant joining the long and growing ranks of unemployed film school graduates. I always felt discouraged by seeing these unhappy souls wait tables and man cash registers around town.

I felt trapped and anxious because I could see no way to break free of my current job so I could move on to something better suited to my education and my tiny, but compelling, film resume. All I knew was that I did not have to commit a felony to feel imprisoned for an unspecified duration.

During this period of malaise, many people told me I should read Louise Hay's *You Can Heal Your Life*. It took me a long time to give in because I could not see the value of a self-help book in overcoming the concrete obstacles besieging me.

The Secret to My Magical Thinking

When I finally relented, *You Can Heal Your Life* unleashed a dormant part of my personality, namely my overly developed sense of magical thinking, or the belief that dramatic life improvements are just days away. Many years passed before I could identify both the magical thinking and my pronounced sense of entitlement as the central instigators of my downfall.

Affirmations: My New Lifestyle

You Can Heal Your Life may be a decent book for those hoping for a spiritual awakening, as long as they do not take everything literally or magnify Hay's advice, as I did.

More specifically, where Hay advises writing out a few affirmations and reciting them twice a day, I operated on the premise that more must certainly be better, especially for novices such as myself. So I typed out four single-spaced pages of affirmations, covering several themes. I wanted to be embarrassingly rich, pencil thin, wildly successful, and deeply in love. I reworded everything so that these demands would be stated in varying ways many times in those four pages. Reciting this mantra six times, twice a day did not cut it after a week. So I tripled the list, and *voilà*, I had 12 pages to read aloud six times, twice a day, and even more often on weekends.

My Secret Headaches and Subconscious Custodian

As a result of all the recitations, excruciating headaches were the norm, as if I were slapping myself upside the head a dozen times each morning, repeating the exercise 10 hours later, then again the next morning, and on and on. Over-the-counter headache medicine may as well have been candy for all the relief it provided.

I eventually understood that these affirmations essentially spoke to my unconscious, which housed all my buried dirt, including unresolved childhood issues. I later discovered that we submerge certain events and sorrows into the protective supervision of our unconscious until we are adequately equipped to handle them. The headaches came about because my all-too-powerful subconscious custodian had no intention of breaching the barricade surrounding this pain, as if to say:

"What the hell does she think she's doing?" Bam. Bam.

"Hey, I'm sleeping over here." Bam. Bam.

"Yo, knucklehead, get a frickin' life." Bam. Bam.

Evidently, this obnoxious gatekeeper had identified a significant gap between the protected material and my readiness to have it revealed in its raw form.

Before I was able to address this unconscious material, some offensive habits erupted, such as casually judging others and trying to control the lives of everyone around me, to name two. These characteristics occupied my consciousness enough to distract me from self-examination. Eventually, I understood that spending all that negative energy on others was not only spiritually counterproductive, but it also alienated the people I cared about.

The Miracle and the Fallout

The highly concentrated protocol of affirmations damaged my life, but the repercussions were not apparent for some time. In the beginning, nothing much happened beyond the throbbing head, but six months later a miracle occurred. I was still living in Canada and had applied three years earlier for permanent American residency through the Green Card lottery. Out of the blue, U.S. Immigration and Naturalization Services contacted me to see if I would still be interested in permanent residency. This seemed like a miracle because I had no idea they would pull names from previous years to fill current quotas.

Moreover, this was the Rolls Royce of all Green Cards. No lawyers were involved and I paid a mere $150 for the required medical exam, fingerprints, and clearance from the Royal Canadian Mounted Police (Canada's version of the FBI). Best of all, I got the green light in four months instead of the usual five or more years. The unexpected opportunity to move to Los Angeles with my new film degree meant I would be able to take advantage of precious opportunities that were not available in Canada. It was a godsend. Or so it seemed at the time.

Offensive Enthusiasm

As a result of this "miracle," my belief in affirmations and the law of attraction became so hideously pronounced that I proselytized with a frightening intensity. At first, people would listen politely, but they avoided me like the plague soon after.

I was completely mystified. "What's the matter with them?" I wondered. "This is a no-brainer." No brains indeed, as I soon discovered.

Falling from Heaven and Burning in Hell

Moving to Los Angeles reminded me of the Charles Dickens passage: "It was the best of times. It was the worst of times." Los Angeles turned out to be the most nourishing and compatible environment for me and I even found a job in Hollywood through a connection in the film industry.

Things had apparently fallen into place according to the law of attraction. I worked for a production company located in a prestigious post-production facility. Surrounded by professionals at the top of their game, I met dozens of people whose names I recognized from multiple movie credits. Better yet, I felt completely in sync with their collective sensibility. I thought I had died and gone to heaven.

However, a two-headed monster soon emerged and threatened my sense of well being. The two producers I worked for were more toxic than anyone I had ever encountered. Their abuses of power made me feel like an undocumented farmhand who was constantly on the verge of exposure by the authorities.

I was in the country legally, of course, but I was working in an industry that did not embrace entry-level workers over the age of 30. I would later discover that successful people in Hollywood almost always started off at the bottom in their early 20s and worked their way up from there.

My inherent vulnerability in this area gave these cavalier men the leverage to treat me like trash and to impose demands that were nearly impossible to fulfill within a given timeframe. By consistently setting me up to fail, these trust-fund-baby producers accomplished two things:

First, I was a convenient scapegoat.

Second, they were leading me down a path to certain employment termination. In the end, I concluded that they had developed serious hiring remorse within a week of my arrival and this was how they dealt with it.

As a result of this war of attrition, I spent more time closing my office door and bawling than I did feeling in control of the situation. The quality of my work began to reflect this ongoing instability and it came as no surprise when I was summarily fired six months later.

I never again worked in Hollywood. It was as though I had been blacklisted. However, I doubt this was the case because my job was relatively insignificant and these two producers were inconsequential within the industry as a whole. Hence, the job-hunting obstacles that followed could not be tied to these men.

Casting Pearls before Swine

Within eight months of my promising arrival in Hollywood, I was pounding the pavement in search of another job commensurate with my education and credentials. My solid resume had no impact whatsoever on potential employers. Their indifference puzzled me because my qualifications should have at least made me a serious contender for numerous positions. Nevertheless, my job searches came up empty and my money kept dwindling.

To make matters worse, Los Angeles in 1991 experienced its worst recession since 1929, according to the local news. As a result, unhappy employees were clinging to their jobs because compelling job opportunities were rare.

I faxed or mailed 100+ resumes in three or four months, yielding a handful of calls and about 20 rejection letters. I also tried employment agencies for temporary and permanent assignments, but my "foreign" experience led some agency representatives to say, "I see here you have no experience in this country," before they quickly escorted me out.

From the beginning, I had organized a system for job searches, with files named:

- Awaiting Response
- Rejection Letters
- Desperate Only
- When Hell Freezes Over.

After two months of "regular" job-hunting, I exhausted the "Desperate Only" file within a week. Jobs requiring lengthy, exhausting commutes and graveyard shifts made up the bulk of this file. I then stared at the papers in the "When Hell Freezes Over" file, featuring menial opportunities. These jobs paid poorly, but the worst part was that they made demands beyond my physical abilities. For example, working as a cashier did not seem *that* bad, but I would have to stand for longer periods than I was able to endure.

No matter how far down I spiraled or how desperate I felt, I *still* had complete faith in the power of affirmations. I believed "it is just a matter of time" and "a miracle is just a day away." I had not connected my relentless decline with my treasured belief in the law of attraction and her twin sister, magical thinking. Years later, when I finally disengaged myself from this vile pairing, I came to two astonishing realizations:

First, faithful compliance with the law of attraction virtually guaranteed manifesting *anything but* my wishes. In my case, this often meant experiencing the direct opposite of my stated goals.[1]

Second, stuffing my head with affirmations meant that little room was left to actually receive good things. Being open and receptive depended on my reserving a spot for new things. More importantly, with most of the real estate in my mind occupied, I failed to make critical connections. For example, I relied on standard job-hunting procedures and may have overlooked less traditional approaches, such as tying in a news story of a new branch opening locally with the company's potential need for my services.

After countless dead ends on the job-hunting front, the phone's deafening silence drove me to find some way to occupy myself other than waiting for calls that did not come. I needed to fill my free time with something meaningful that would take my mind off my troubles and away from the stress that was growing exponentially.

Consciousness Overhaul at the Los Angeles Public Library

Between job interviews, I discovered a treasure trove of metaphysical material in the central L.A. library. At this point, my unwavering belief in the law of attraction—coupled with the panic I felt about my situation—drew me to books supplementing Louise Hay's *You Can Heal Your Life*. I rationalized that I had either misunderstood Hay or that *You Can Heal Your Life* had not adequately covered reversals of fortune.

In the end, all the subsequent get-rich-quick and law-of-attraction books left me as hungry for guidance as I had been before. So, while I was doing temp work to sustain me, I branched out and found magnificent material unrelated to the law of attraction, including books about:

- Mysticism
- Eastern religions
- Comparative religions
- Consciousness
- Enlightenment
- Free will
- Karma
- Reincarnation
- The afterlife
- The soul
- Scientific paradigms for spirituality
- Transformation
- The healing of childhood issues
- Jungian psychology
- The temporary madness associated with spiritual growth spurts
- The spiritual aspects of:
    - Our purpose in life
    - Dreams
    - Suffering and dark nights of the soul
    - Death and dying
    - Suicide.

These new perspectives made me understand spirituality in a brand new way. I took copious notes and used bibliographies to guide me to deeper material until a fresh context emerged: I had consumed so many powerful perspectives on the above-mentioned topics that discarding the law of attraction actually seemed feasible. This exercise radically altered my thinking and realigned my priorities in several ways:

First, I saw that the accumulation of wealth may be an accomplishment of sorts, but it has nothing to do with spiritual development.

Second, I perceived my place in the big picture more clearly. Instead of comparing myself only to those in my own milieu, I saw myself as a citizen of the planet. Over time, this meant that I felt connected to everyone, including people who embraced alienating cultures and strange traditions. I was forced to conclude that I was much better off than many others around the world, despite the financial challenges facing me at that time.

Third, I understood that I had spent a lifetime being ruled by a sense of entitlement, which I later discovered had lured me to the law of attraction in the first place.

Fourth, a sober assessment of my current circumstances eventually produced gratitude for my life as it was. This allowed me to accept my substandard situation when things did not fall into place easily.

Fifth, as my perspective shifted, an unprecedented outlook surfaced: For the first time, I identified with people whose aspirations had to be postponed or canceled so they could deal with basic survival needs or pressing responsibilities, such as parenting.

Sixth, as time went on, I discovered that these individuals probably represented the majority of the population, as I had met precious few people who were actually living their dreams. As long as I had clung to my sense of entitlement, I had remained completely oblivious to these particular individuals, who surrounded me on a daily basis. By shedding the entitlement, I could finally relate to others in a way not possible before.

Seventh, my comprehension of humanity became even deeper when I realized that everyone's journey is unique and includes mysterious elements that are beyond my ability to understand. Hence, my strong inclination to offhandedly judge others also disintegrated.

This whole process mimicked a domino effect and spanned several years.

Sinking Further into Poverty

Though my mind and spirit underwent a massive renovation, my life continued to decline financially. I faced eviction and destitution so profound that it took me 17 years to reach the first stages of financial recovery. Over the years, I was briefly homeless and sometimes had to make do with annual incomes as low as $5,000. I was far too often unemployed, underemployed, or financially dependent on others.

Several other areas of my life were also adversely affected. For example, I went through junky cars faster than toothpaste. In a 10-year span, my rust buckets died so quickly that none of them ever qualified for an oil change. As time wore on, the periods without cars grew longer and longer.

Living with the Crazies

During this period, the people around me changed drastically. My closest friends stood by me, but I suddenly accumulated more insane acquaintances than a psychiatrist with a thriving practice.

During one two-year stretch, I worked in a telemarketing boiler room with a variety of colorful individuals. Several people showed up to work with twigs and leaves stuck to the backs of their clothing and hair. My coworkers included the certifiably mentally ill, as well as a wide assortment of bottom feeders. Drug dealers, addicts, porno-filmmaker wannabes, and convicted child molesters surrounded me on a daily basis. The advanced alcoholics openly discussed the various states of collapse afflicting their internal organs. "The doctor gave me two years tops," a coworker said. "My pancreas is shot."

One day at lunch hour, two drug-dealing coworkers were arrested in the company parking lot. Four managers (who were their best customers) chipped in for their bail and the drug dealers returned to work a few hours later.

At the same time, I was renting a room in the house of a woman who frequently signed up for extended stays at psychiatric facilities for treatment of her alcohol-induced psychosis. She always referred to these crises as a need for "medication adjustments." She typically recruited new renters there, rendering me the only person in this crowded rooming house who was not using psychotropic drugs. Between work and home, I sometimes became so stressed out that I could not appreciate my own sanity because I failed to detect it.

For the most part, I felt so overwhelmed by these characters that I camped out in their psychological territory more often than I care to recall. I learned that solid footing within the realm of mental health is quite tenuous and that extreme situations can convert stable mental soil into psychological quicksand. In my case, *terra firma* was restored, but not until my spiritual compass made its debut at long last. Once I gained enough spiritual clarity, the law of attraction dissolved in my consciousness and mental stability resurfaced.

Medical Debility and Absent Men

On the health front, an alarming deterioration emerged, which eventually put me in a wheelchair. I was diagnosed with three herniated disks, which paved the way to advanced osteoarthritis and spinal stenosis, or a narrowing of the spine. At first, the herniated disks only caused me to limp due to the sciatic pain shooting down my leg. However, because the herniations were misdiagnosed for more than three years, osteoarthritis set in and my spinal column began to narrow. These conditions emerged 20+ years before they should have and each one is progressive, incurable, and produces unpleasant complications over time.

The osteoarthritis ravaged my knees and my range of motion is now so curtailed that my legs are comfortable only at a 90-degree angle, or in the sitting position. I can sleep on my back only if my knees are propped up. When I walk, I am more stooped over than any elderly person I have ever seen. Whether I sit, lie down, or walk a few feet, my body appears to be frozen in the "S" position, like Bernie's fixed *rigor mortis* pose in *Weekend at Bernie's* (1993).

During the healthy times when I exercised at least six hours per week for decades, I could boast about impressive cholesterol and blood pressure numbers. I later found out that some doctors call this "fat and fit."

I did not foresee that the hour-long walks I took most days were inflicting a terrible punishment on my muscular-skeletal system. Over time, I taxed my joints almost to the point of extinction. Therefore, the regime I had designed to circumvent obesity-related issues was the very cause of my medical downfall.

To this day, my medical situation remains dark and ominous. All things considered, my medical age is at least 20 years older than my chronological age. In fact, I have seen plenty of 80-somethings in better shape than I am. Despite all this, I feel obligated to take full responsibility for my life in a wheelchair. It used to be easy to blame all the doctors who misdiagnosed my condition, but I was the real culprit; I persistently maintained a high weight, which became my undoing.

During this five-year span of rapid medical decline, very few rays of sunshine poked through the clouds in other areas. My romantic life vanished and my weight continued to fluctuate between fat and fatter. On every front, I was constantly deciding between bad and worse. So much for "rich, thin, successful, and in love."

If Only I Had Hip Waders

Instead of moving toward the goals outlined by my affirmations, my experiences were nasty and unprecedented, pulling me further and further away. Worse still, I had to slog through the polluted waters that now comprised my life without the benefit of previous life experiences to draw from. Nothing had prepared me for any of this. The only certainty was that the law of attraction had a sickening, bleak side that nobody ever talked about.

The Secret Horror Show

It goes without saying that I was mortified when *The Secret* burst onto the scene. At first, I could not believe what I was seeing on *The Oprah Winfrey Show*. I reacted on so many levels at once that my brain nearly short-circuited.

Shortly afterwards, I realized that while I functioned well in my daily life, every time I tried to discuss *The Secret* I was rendered mute. I simply could not translate what was screaming in my head into intelligible conversation. *The Secret* pushed so many buttons that it was almost a week after *The Oprah Winfrey Show* before I could verbalize anything related to *The Secret*. Then it was like a monsoon. At that point I could not be silenced, so I wrote about it.

Chapter 2

Snake Oil, P.T. Barnum, and *The Secret*

According to *The Secret's* acknowledgements page, *The Secret* is a corporation called T.S. Production LLC, with CEO Bob Rainone at the helm. A former IBM salesman and telecom executive, Rainone neither wrote nor edited any part of *The Secret*, but he is clearly a marketing brainiac.[2]

While developing *The Secret,* his company employed:

- Editor Rhonda Byrne, who created *The Secret*
- Two website managers
- A four-person production team
- Twenty-four contributors, whose qualifications range from "life coach" to "visionary."[3]

In an odd way, *The Secret* has probably made publishing history: Instead of a lonely author tapping away at a keyboard, surrounded by piles of papers and books, we get content by committee for maximum marketing effect. In addition, *The Secret's* remarkable dust jacket looks similar to *The Da Vinci Code's*, while the interior graphic design and parchment-like appearance harkens back to the *Dead Sea Scrolls*.

Every word has been carefully examined and tweaked with two things in mind: Marketing and money, with an emphasis on get-rich-quick. "Get-rich-quick" has a double meaning here: It refers to the reader's interest in instant wealth as well as to *The Secret's* accumulation of massive revenues at lightning speed.

In September 2007, the company launched Phase II of its marketing plan, including a book sequel and another DVD, and a third book is in the works.[4] And let's not forget the speaking engagements. James Ray, one of the book's contributors, commands $3,495/person for his weekend seminars.[5] *The Secret* has also been a godsend to Rhonda Byrne, who personally accumulated $12 million between July 1, 2006 to June 30, 2007, according to *Forbes*.

CEO Bob Rainone blatantly told a reporter that *The Secret*'s "wealth enhancement" was deliberately emphasized.[6] Anyone with the slightest inkling about spiritual development knows that amassing riches has nothing to do with our spiritual well being.

On top of everything, the book does not hold just a measly copyright, but has a registered trademark as well, implying that merchandising was planned all along. [7] And if that is not enough, CBS Corporation owns both Simon & Schuster (publisher of *The Secret*) and King World, the company that produces *The Oprah Winfrey Show*, which featured two one-hour episodes about *The Secret*.[8]

The Genie-in-a-Bottle Effect

One of the many offensive aspects of *The Secret* is its promise that absolutely anything envisioned can be manifested, as if God grants each and every wish just like a genie in a bottle. However, practicing the law of attraction promises *limitless* wishes instead of just the three offered by a genie. Indeed, *The Secret* DVD even features Aladdin and his lamp with the tag line: "Your wish is my command."

Visualizations, affirmations, and prayers fall under the umbrella of "petitions to God." *The Secret* fails to acknowledge that *unanswered* petitions are the norm because fulfillment of the most dramatic or life-changing prayers usually conflicts with our karmic standing and/or our purpose in life, among other things. This means that we can babble affirmations and visualize day in and day out for years on end and get nothing. Or, worse, our lives can deteriorate in the very area in which we seek healing. This reversal not only happened to me, but I have seen it with others as well.

Clotaire Rapaille and the Reptilian Brain

The Secret's mega success causes many of us to scratch our heads, wondering why an otherwise intelligent person would swallow the law of attraction hook, line, and sinker.

As cultural anthropologist and psychiatrist Clotaire Rapaille (1941-) points out, this contradiction between mass appeal and mindless content can be explained. Though Rapaille has not publicly analyzed *The Secret's* success, he does scrutinize similar conflicts in other areas of our lives. For example, a man may be vocally supportive of energy conservation and other environmental issues, but he may still purchase a gas-guzzler such as the Hummer. More commonly, some of us study nutrition labels at the supermarket, but we then eat six times the recommended amount of the low-sugar or reduced-fat selections. This opposition between word and action is the product of our "reptilian brain," which, according to Rapaille, dominates our psyches until we are about seven years old.[9]

Rapaille explains the illogical behavior by pointing out that even as adults we occasionally set aside our rational mind when making purchases. Instead, our reptilian brain controls some of our buying decisions, particularly the ones involving luxury items. This means that the imprints we receive as preschoolers sometimes carry more weight in influencing our adult behavior than does our rational mind.

Reptilian Imprints

Childhood imprints may include icons such as the military. For example, a marine's son may have played with toy soldiers for many years. As an adult, the son still has positive associations with military symbols.

An imprint might also refer to a smell, such as the aroma of brewing coffee, which has been experienced on a daily basis since birth.[10] All of this occurs subliminally, usually with no direct influence from others.

The imprints triggered by *The Secret* relate to our preschool sense of entitlement and the innate magical thinking to which we revert when our reptilian brain dominates. Furthermore, *The Secret* appears to have struck a chord within our *cultural* reptilian brain, which desires the wealth necessary to purchase luxury items. This is the only explanation that can account for *The Secret's* success and it certainly illuminates how I succumbed to the law of attraction in the 1980s in such a pig-headed fashion.

People who face criticism for an ill-advised reptilian decision often make little sense when they defend their actions, especially in light of the sober, intelligent way in which they might approach non-reptilian issues. This means that loved ones do not stand a chance of reasoning with a person whose reptilian side is the only one listening.

Reptiles in Denial

Whether choices are challenged or not, denial plays an important role in justifying such irrational decisions.

Likewise, denial prevents fervent believers in the law of attraction from objectively examining the countless promises of wish fulfillment that dominate *The Secret*. If these readers took a good hard look at all the people they have known throughout the years, they would see that rough patches and long postponed dreams are the rule, not the exception. Furthermore, if law-of-attraction practitioners made a list, they would soon discover that successful people run the gamut from grouchy cynics to those with the sunniest dispositions, yet they all achieved success in much the same way: By working very hard and taking scary risks. Realizing big dreams is a lengthy and difficult process, typically involving tons of energy and plenty of setbacks along the way.

Of course, some of us accept life as it has been laid out in front of us. *The Secret* authors probably believe that these people still need to be enlightened by the law of attraction. Nevertheless, acceptance of life's circumstances—which have absolutely nothing to do with what we wanted in our 20s and 30s—is actually a signpost of significant spiritual maturity.

The Power of Acceptance

Most of us experience meager, mediocre, or trying circumstances in at least one aspect of our daily lives. Through acceptance—and by doing our best with the situation at hand—we not only make our lives better within these parameters, but we slowly and steadily grow spiritually as well.

I imagine the Scales of Justice, with wealth on one side and spiritual development on the other. *The Secret* blatantly disregards half of this balancing act. Of course, wealth and spirituality are not mutually exclusive and we *can* theoretically achieve both. However, greed—and pursuits driven by a sense of entitlement—pretty much wipe out the possibility of any spiritual growth during a period dominated by such quests. A person preoccupied with manifesting wealth is doing *anything but* taking care of matters deemed important from a spiritual standpoint.

Unsung Heroes

In the movie *A Bronx Tale* (1993), Lorenzo (Robert DeNiro) is a straight-laced bus driver who has developed a profound level of acceptance. His son is slowly being seduced by the grandiose lifestyle generated by neighborhood mobsters. Lorenzo can only offer the child a Spartan home, which clashes with the fancy cars and houses owned by the criminals. At one point, Lorenzo says that it takes courage to face his job and his life every day. Lorenzo also believes that real men always honor responsibilities.

Lorenzo shows us that a seemingly unremarkable life can be infused with integrity and dignity. Indeed, people like Lorenzo are the real role models, but few of us recognize that. As a result, our current cultural climate and collective mentality are ultra receptive to *The Secret's* core message.

The Law of Attraction and Large Groups

One way to assess *The Secret*'s gaping omissions is to look at large groups, such as:

- The populations of disadvantaged third-world countries
- The mentally ill, or otherwise disenfranchised
- The disfigured
- The permanently disabled
- The terminally ill who occupy thousands of hospice beds all over the world.

The Secret's contributors would dismiss all this suffering as negative thinking or as a lack of knowledge about the law of attraction. *The Secret's* authors apparently refuse to acknowledge that *life happens*, that people get sick and die, and that the cards we have been dealt vary tremendously. These cards differ among us and they also change at different points in our own lives. In contrast, *The Secret* prefers to blame the victim.

Furthermore, a stubborn refusal to acknowledge the dual nature of reality runs through *The Secret* like an incurable virus. At different times in our lives, we face sickness and health, joy and sorrow, lack and abundance, and so on. I cannot recall a single optimist who has not experienced these cycles in one form or another. Nevertheless, *The Secret* would have us believe that we can avoid all the low points with sustained positive thinking.

In truth, we constantly move in and out of different phases. Both desirable and painful times come to an end eventually. We are relieved to let go of the hardship and are saddened by the end of a really great situation or relationship. In both cases, new people and circumstances emerge to fill the voids. These cycles structure our lives and guide us through events and relationships. Even so, *The Secret* prefers to dwell on stunning improvements that it promises will materialize, usually in 30 days or less.

The Secret's claims consistently clash with observation and experience. After living in Hell for nearly two decades, I personally see positive thinking as useful, but overrated. One possible benefit seems to be compelling: Positive thinkers enjoy life more than cynics. Or do they?

Optimists and Pessimists

Interestingly, pessimists tell us that they never get their hopes up, so they rarely feel disappointed. This tells me that optimists and pessimists employ different survival skills. And that is it. We all erect protective barriers, so the pessimist's coping strategies are every bit as viable as the optimist's. If the law of attraction worked the way *The Secret's* authors suggest, then negative thinkers would never draw good things into their lives. Ever.

I have seen the opposite time and again. One side of the discussion is populated by individuals we may recognize:

- People with low self-esteem attracting rewarding love relationships
- Depressed individuals getting an impressive promotion
- Cynics enjoying a huge windfall
- Pathologically insecure entrepreneurs with thriving businesses
- Pessimistic and surly middle managers who alienate everyone in their orbit. However, they never seem to get into trouble and appear to have a relatively firm grip on job security
- Negative thinkers who mystify doctors with 20-year remissions from stage-four cancer.

On the other side, we have:

- Confident, mentally healthy people who fail miserably at love
- Hard workers with glowing personalities who are often overlooked for the promotions they deserve

- Optimists who trudge through life with few visible rewards
- Hopeful and savvy people whose business ventures fail time and again
- Self-assured and once successful executives who find themselves in a Hell of low-end jobs with single-digit hourly wages and pesky micromanagers
- Positive thinkers who die of stage-two cancer within a year.

Positive Thinking and Surviving Cancer

While we are on the topic of surviving cancer, let's discuss Dr.. Jimmie Holland's article called *The Tyranny of Positive Thinking*, which considers the harsh realities facing cancer patients. Holland bases his theories on his 24 years of experience counseling patients at Memorial Sloan-Kettering Cancer Center in Manhattan.[11]

Holland believes that low self-esteem and a poor attitude have nothing to do with either attracting cancer or surviving it. He asserts that lifestyle issues—such as smoking, poor diet, lack of exercise, and several other vices—are much stronger contributors. Holland also believes that even positive thinkers who lead relatively healthy and smoke-free lives can develop cancer.

Holland chastises the "positive thinking police" for not allowing cancer patients to feel blue about the horrors of chemotherapy. Their censorious attitude implies that a negative reaction to the treatments will only help tumors to grow. Holland concedes that anxiety may adversely affect a patient's recovery, but he believes that while "stress does affect the immune system, there is no evidence that the blips produced are in the range of those that would affect tumor growth."[12]

Holland has observed negative thinkers thriving for decades after a terminal diagnosis and he feels that cancer patients should make no alteration to their thinking. Whether we are optimists or pessimists, staying true to ourselves seems to be what is most important to Holland. "Identify your own beliefs about the mind-body connection and use them as they are comfortable for you, based on your temperament and your natural ways of coping", Holland advises.[13]

The New Medicine

I fully subscribe to Holland's viewpoint and a PBS documentary called *The New Medicine* (2006) sheds more light. Many solid research findings about the value of guided visualizations in reducing pain and about the adverse effects of stress on healing inform *The New Medicine*. Evidently, stress activates cortisol and adrenalin production, which in turn lowers our immune system. Therefore, sustained stress predisposes us to illness and slower healing.[14]

A pair of researchers had been captivated by reports of soldiers recovering from serious wounds. They examined documentation that showed soldiers injured in a winning battle faring much better than those with comparable wounds incurred during a combat they had lost.

Inspired by this report, these researchers devised a study about stress and healing. They observed women who shared many similarities, such as age, income level, etc. Half of them were primary caretakers for an Alzheimer's patient while the rest were not caretakers. The researchers believed that the caretakers underwent far more stress than the non-caretakers and they expected to find differences in their bodies' abilities to heal a small wound.

The doctors punctured each subject's skin with a tiny circular device and periodically took photos of the wound as it healed. Not surprisingly, the pictures showed that the non-caretakers completed the healing nine days earlier (on average) than the caretakers. Extrapolations of this study also indicate a sharp reduction in post-op recovery times for patients who practiced stress-reduction techniques prior to the surgery.

The New Medicine also showed how chronic-pain patients benefit from guided visualizations. In two cases, guided visualizations meant the difference between nearly non-functioning and functioning well, due to a sharp reduction in pain.

The New Medicine versus Dr.. Holland

We can pinpoint a subtle distinction between Holland's theories and those put forth in *The New Medicine* because the paths taken by the respective patients vary. For example, the period of chemotherapy is wretched enough, but the cancer patient also faces a long period of uncertainty afterwards. In contrast, the chronic-pain patient really has nothing to lose by trying guided visualizations and potentially much to gain. In addition, *The New Medicine* treatments never produce pain or discomfort, whereas chemotherapy usually does.

Because of the many impressive examples cited by *The New Medicine*, I feel that we should rethink the whole issue of hounding sick people into positive thinking. For example, insisting on positive thinking for its own sake seems to be a pointless directive at best, when compared to *The New Medicine's* methods for pain management and stress reduction.

In general, browbeating people into adopting a brighter outlook does nothing except to shove that person's existential pain underground. This means that the bully's next encounter with that person is sure to be met with counterfeit optimism and the bully may have unintentionally alienated the person for good.

If we are interested in retaining friends and acquaintances, I also believe that recommending stress-reduction or guided-visualization techniques to an ailing person is far more constructive than constantly insisting on a positive outlook, as such pressure to change probably magnifies the patient's feelings of isolation.

If I ever have a sick friend whose energy is depleted by her illness, I will research the latest techniques on her behalf. Perhaps I can present her with some options, such as local groups that focus on similar strategies, or books she might find helpful. She may not be well enough to take advantage of these suggestions, but at least she may view this as an act of friendship and inclusion.

This discussion illustrates how much some of us need to re-examine our lives. Reverting to common sense often presents the best solutions.

The New Medicine versus *The Secret*

The techniques put forth in *The New Medicine* illustrate viable applications of positive thinking because a patient's willingness is a necessary precursor to success. Unlike *The Secret's* main theme of simply wishing for a full recovery that should then miraculously occur, *The New Medicine* concentrates on mindfulness, focus, and living in the moment.

The goal is greater relaxation, which could produce a reduction of vexing symptoms. Therefore, *The New Medicine's* techniques focus on a much smaller and more realistic outcome than *The Secret* does. Indeed, mountains of irrefutable research spanning decades have fortified the connection between stress reduction and desirable outcomes for our health. However, Rhonda Byrne's 18-day research marathon (according to Byrne's interview in *Newsweek*) produced flawed and unconvincing results for *The Secret*.

When comparing *The New Medicine* to *The Secret*, we find polar opposites in their respective approaches. *The Secret* routinely over-promises and under-delivers, while doctors featured in *The New Medicine* guarantee nothing except the chance to reduce pain and stress. They also emphasize that the treatments in no way represent a cure for the underlying illness, though the techniques may improve quality-of-life issues and increase life expectancy in some cases.

As a side note, I viewed *The New Medicine* a few days before seeing *The Secret* DVD. The two productions clashed so dramatically that I suspected they were produced in different galaxies.

The Secret DVD

A slick production, *The Secret* DVD shows us the contemporary version of snake oil at its finest. *The Secret* DVD is neither a feature film nor a documentary and can only be fairly characterized as an expensively produced infomercial, featuring hundreds of extras.

My favorite parts include the quotes from famous people. As words are written on the screen, they are also spoken in a hushed whisper, as if a well-guarded, clandestine secret is being revealed at long last. One such quote comes from Albert Einstein:

> Imagination is everything. It is the preview of life's coming attractions.
>
> Albert Einstein
> *The Secret*

Einstein's sentiment may resemble *The Secret's* philosophy, but including it as corroboration of the law of attraction misleads us. Granted, all great things must be thought of first, but the opposite is simply not true: Thinking about wonderful events or situations does not make them happen. We can nurture dreams for decades and *never* see them materialize.

For example, I know one woman who finally accumulated enough money to start her dream business, but by then too many similar businesses were already well established. As the adage goes, she was "a day late...."

This discussion calls to mind the Serenity Prayer adopted by Alcoholics Anonymous in 1942, which elegantly eclipses *The Secret's* principal message:

> God grant us the serenity to accept the things we cannot change, the courage to change the things we can, and the wisdom to know the difference.
>
> Saint Francis of Assisi

Hurricane Katrina and 9/11

If we accept *The Secret's* premise, then the casualties and surviving family members of both Hurricane Katrina and 9/11 were all negative thinkers who attracted these tragedies. Furthermore, people who worked at the Twin Towers, but who were not there when the planes crashed, must have been practicing the law of attraction, along with all those who left New Orleans before Katrina hit. I guarantee that people within *all* these groups represent the entire scope of thinking, from negative to positive, from confident to insecure, and all the other polar opposites we can conjure.

Life's Intricacies

The Secret refuses to acknowledge the staggering complexities and nearly endless variables woven into our individual lives. Instead, these authors deliver reptilian simplicity on each and every page.

Among dozens of irksome oversights, the spiritual value of making sacrifices for our loved ones is sorely absent. We face uncomfortable decision-making during these frustrating times: We are torn between improving our lives in some way and attending to the needs of a loved one. The next example clearly demonstrates that we can experience long periods of these either/or situations.

I knew a couple who easily envisioned success for their planned Internet business. They decided to live more frugally and to save as much money as possible so they could launch the business. They were a bit pressed for time because they wanted to be profitable several years before their adolescent children graduated from high school and needed money for college. By anyone's standards, this couple was on track and had exhaustively researched their subject. Money was the only missing element.

When the couple had accumulated half the funds, their son had a football-related accident. Some of his treatments were not covered by insurance and the bills quickly ate up the family's savings until they began to sink into debt. The son's medical crisis passed, but it took the parents two years just to clear up the debt load and save a bit of money again. Then something happened to their daughter and the cycle was repeated. What would *The Secret* authors say about this family? We know the drill by now.

By pressing on with their law-of-attraction platitudes, these authors fail to acknowledge the value of loving sacrifice. True, in the story above, the parents repeatedly had to table their dream, but they intentionally used the funds for their son's treatments instead of cutting corners on his care so they could preserve their nest egg.

Expressions of love top the list of spiritual values. In fact, the more we experience love in all its magnificent forms, the richer our lives become, regardless of our sometimes paltry net worth.

Here We Go Again

Many bestsellers about the law of attraction were published during its 1980s incarnation, but no single title was ever as successful as *The Secret.*

We already know how disastrous this belief system was for me in particular. In the upcoming chapters, we will see just how potentially destructive it can be in terms of personal spiritual development.

Timing Is Everything

If nothing else, I have learned that timing is everything. The authors of *The Secret* surely owe their success in part to appealing to a different generation, two decades or so after the last fad. However, millions of us still remember our own gullibility 20+ years ago. Fortunately, most of us were lucky enough to quickly understand that the law of attraction simply does not work.

However, some patients with life-threatening illnesses reportedly abandoned medical treatment in favor of the "positive thinking" techniques put forth by dozens of authors in the 1980s. People this gullible represent a miniscule percentage of readers, but even a single person misled to such an extent is one too many.

According to Wikipedia, solid research findings reveal that supplanting medical care with positive thinking works for minor ailments only. For serious diseases, these alternatives should be considered solely as enhancements to conventional medical care. Perhaps this is why *The*

Secret's copyright page features a lengthy disclaimer, which states in part: [The book's advice] "should not replace consultation with a competent healthcare professional."[15]

Oprah, *The Secret,* and Medical Issues

After several weeks of reruns, *The Oprah Winfrey Show* returned with new episodes on March 26, 2007. Just three weeks earlier, Oprah had aired her second show devoted to *The Secret.*

The very first item in the new show featured an email about *The Secret.* A viewer named Kim Tinkham wrote in about her stage-three breast cancer diagnosis. Three doctors had said she needed surgery within the month, but Tinkham opted for a non-invasive, more natural approach after reading *The Secret.* Instead of the recommended partial radical mastectomy of the right breast and lymph nodes, Tinkham preferred to eat only organic foods and work with a nutritionist to remove toxins from her body. Finally, Tinkham put up dark curtains in her bedroom and made sure she slept at least seven or eight hours each night.[16]

Oprah's conversation with Tinkham showed that the woman might have made a reasonably well-informed decision. However, I could not help noticing the contrast between Tinkham's rational on-air demeanor and the contents of the email. Tinkham's letter to Oprah credited *The Secret* for her move away from conventional medical help. Tinkham also said that she did a lot of doctor shopping before finding one who agreed to monitor her for six months while she used natural remedies in conjunction with the law of attraction. This meant that months would pass before Tinkham would know if she was on the right track. Neither Oprah nor Tinkham mentioned that six months is potentially enough time for stage-three cancer to advance to stage four. At that point, it would have spread to other organs and would be considered "end-stage."

To her credit, Oprah pointed out that one could incorporate the law of attraction *and* seek tried-and-true treatment at the same time. Oprah's restrained demeanor suggested that she was in no way supportive of

Tinkham's decision. We can only imagine the panic that might have rippled through the Harpo Studios' legal department when Tinkham's email arrived.

Immediately after her conversation with Tinkham, Oprah addressed the camera to tone down her once infectious eagerness about *The Secret.*

From the time of this broadcast to the end of 2007, virtually no meaningful trace of *The Secret* could be found in the media. To my knowledge, the summer 2007 reruns of *The Oprah Winfrey Show, Larry King Live,* and *The Ellen DeGeneres Show* have not included *The Secret,* though during the year all of them had broadcast shows devoted to the book.

Despite the absence of noteworthy media attention by September 2007, Amazon.com still ranked *The Secret* tenth in overall sales and number one in three separate subject categories. Also in September 2007, *The Secret* resurfaced on bestseller lists, such as *The New York Times* (at number one) and the *Chicago Tribune* (at number three).

September 2007 appears to have been *The Secret's* final peak month. Amazon's ranking of *The Secret* slipped in October until the book dropped to 37 in November 2007. A similar decline in November was also reflected by the *Chicago Tribune*, which ranked the book at eight while *The New York Times* demoted *The Secret* to fourth place.

Of course, even these lower statistics would be quite desirable to publishers and authors alike. Nevertheless, *The Secret's* stranglehold on such sustained high rankings for such a long time tells us more about the culture we live in than it does about *The Secret's* literary value.

The Law of Attraction Now versus the 1980s

For the most part, the 1980s law-of-attraction authors had the good sense to at least add supplementary material of value, affording the reader some kind of spiritual anchor. As I look back now, I suspect that quite a few of these authors had independent material at the ready and simply tacked on the law of attraction due to its overwhelming popularity. Such is not the case with *The Secret*, which blithely masquerades as Divinely inspired scripture. For many reasons, this ruse troubles me greatly.

First, our cultural tendency towards quick fixes sets many of us up to unconditionally endorse *The Secret*. Indeed, with more than six million books and DVDs sold by September 2007, *The Secret* may top 12 million units by the end of 2008, despite its shrinking stature at the end of 2007.[17]

Twelve million may be a reasonable estimate due to the powerful combination of countless speaking engagements and the unprecedented avalanche effect that gained force once the book reached its tipping point in early 2007. By March 2007, 1.7 million books and 1.5 million DVDs had been sold and nearly three million more units flew off the shelves in the next six months.[18]

The second aspect of this subterfuge refers to the many readers who will accept *The Secret's* shallow assertions as viable metaphysical advice.

Third, the really great metaphysical authors get lost in the superficial shuffle. Past and present researchers have created a formidable body of work for serious seekers. Of course, *The Secret* will not sway sincere readers searching for substantial material, but the uninitiated may view *The Secret* as the real deal. Moreover, *The Secret* effectively contaminates the whole field of study. Angry detractors already use *The Secret* to reduce metaphysical research as a whole to "psychobabble and bull****."

Finally, *The Secret* claims that the law of attraction dates back centuries and names international historical figures who have supposedly benefited from it. Oddly enough, my research disputes this claim, despite Rhonda Byrne's assertion that she read "hundreds" of books and articles in an 18-day stretch.[19]

The History of the Law of Attraction

My investigation indicates that the law of attraction was born and raised in the United States and has thrived for fewer than 175 years, while *The Secret* claims that global interest spans thousands of years.

I traced the philosophy's roots back to Phineas Parkhurst Quimby (born in New Hampshire; 1802-1866). By the 1890s, his work was dubbed "New Thought." This morphed into "Science of Mind," a term coined by Ernest Holmes (born in Maine; 1887-1960), who continued the tradition.

Norman Vincent Peale (born in Ohio; 1898-1993) revived the craze in the 1950s with *The Power of Positive Thinking*. This enormously popular book promoted the law of attraction from a Christian perspective, while subsequent incarnations usually favored a nondenominational approach.

Louise Hay (born in California; 1927-) reverted to Ernest Holmes' material and ran with it. In 1976, Hay published *Heal Your Body*, but the 1984 release of *You Can Heal Your Life* established Hay as (arguably) the initiator of the law-of-attraction craze in the 1980s.

Dozens of other authors jumped on the bandwagon, offering material of varying quality and value. Also in the 1980s, publishers introduced "New Thought" as a fresh category to reflect this rapidly growing field.

Some of these authors, including Hay, still have quite a loyal following. These writers presumably owe their staying power to moving beyond the law of attraction in its purest form. In the 1980s, they typically supplemented this concept with either a novel context or inspired improvements, all of which diluted the potentially dangerous message generated by discussions of the law of attraction alone.

Now that we understand the historical context, let's move on to the specifics of how the law of attraction interacts with other Universal laws.

Part 2

More Universal Laws

Chapter 3

The Laws Governing External Sources of Suffering

As you may have already noticed, *The Secret* and other books about the law of attraction trivialize the complexity of the human experience and consistently fail to acknowledge other crucial factors, such as periods of severe anguish.

Suffering overtakes our spirits and manifests in so many ways that by the time we are 40 its imprint on our psyche is as unique as our DNA profile. In one form or another, hardship is endemic to the human experience. Interestingly, Buddhists look through the prism of suffering and compassion to bolster their spiritual understanding and to fortify their acceptance of the way life works.

After considerable contemplation, I can only explain the purpose of suffering by describing what happens in its absence. When we go through intervals of contentment in most areas of our lives, we often conclude—unconsciously at least—that "if it ain't broke, don't fix it." Then we stop working on our spiritual development.

These periods of grace become a respite from our main spiritual goal of learning. The intermissions are like holidays because we are blessed with low-maintenance situations for awhile and are not expected to work on spiritual advancement at all. The natural tendency is to take these breaks for granted and grow complacent, because we are not motivated to challenge ourselves during the good times, just as we lack incentive while on vacation.

The easier interludes occur between much longer periods when we are more attuned to faltering areas in our own lives. At such times, we rarely connect our distress with opportunities to learn lessons. Even so, most of us understand this correlation in hindsight. Looking back imparts a degree of clarity compared to the murky nature of the actual hardship as we go through it.

The variety of potential issues we face can be enormous, particularly when we factor in our observations of what other people have to endure. Let's discuss some of these now.

Difficulties without Resolution

Some kinds of suffering offer no feasible way out. Let's consider a long-term situation with no obvious resolution. For example, a four-year-old girl—who lost both parents in a car accident—spent the next 14 years in the harsh world of the foster-care system. She missed the opportunities for education that would have been available had her parents lived. She was also deprived of quality parental care and concern.

By the time she turned 21, she was lost and confused and felt like damaged goods. The burden of such wounds may have been greater for her than most of us bear at that age. Nevertheless, she really has no choice but to make the most of her situation and go on. As an adult, she must mull over opportunities as they arise and make decisions for better or for worse. In addition, her unusual circumstances and added burdens do not exempt her from fulfilling her spiritual mandate.

Adversities with Possible Solutions

Another type of suffering points to situations that theoretically can be resolved, such as financial distress. When we encounter monetary difficulties, we immediately look for solutions. We tackle the obvious things first: We might get a second mortgage, find another job, and try to collect old debts. However, if circumstances show that our efforts are in vain, or we once again run out of money, we must look for different approaches. If these also fail and bill collectors badger us all day long, we may sink into despair.

Despite contrary indicators, these dilemmas encompass a positive element: All this activity galvanizes our spiritual side, though we rarely perceive the misery as a means to eventually reach the point of facing the lessons we need to learn. Our success depends on our willingness to confront longstanding issues. Accordingly, this process—including the attendant adversities—may be repeated many times throughout our lives.

Mellowing over the Years

Both William Styron's *Darkness Visible* and Carl Jung's *The Portable Jung* refer to a "knock at the door" starting as early as 35 years of age. These faintly discernible mental "knocks" remind us of hearing a neighbor's alarm clock: They are just loud enough to be heard, but not resounding enough to be characterized as a "wakeup call."

If we ignore the gentle rapping we become predisposed to depression and midlife crisis. At this point, repressing issues—whose time is ripe for revelation—carries the potential for woefulness or a frenzied attempt to reclaim our lost youth.

These subtle, slippery middle-age cues are barely perceptible and we easily set them aside even after numerous prompts. However, we are spiritually obligated to take a long, hard look at our life as it is at that moment, with both the beautiful and the hideous in sharp focus.

On the ugly front, specific situations, ideas, and behaviors must go, particularly if they have never worked or if they have outlived their usefulness. If we take refuge in escapism or denial, we not only postpone the inevitable, but we also negatively influence our daily functioning and inadvertently sabotage our real-life goals. If we fail to respond by the time we are 50, we can turn into unsightly distortions of our younger selves. Carl Jung warns that if we do not learn as opportunities arise we become unbearably pigheaded:

> One's cherished principles and convictions, especially the moral ones, begin to harden and to grow incessantly rigid until somewhere around the age of 50 a period of intolerance and fanaticism is reached.
>
> Carl Jung
> *The Portable Jung*

Jung goes on to explain that we react as though these principles seem "endangered" to us, so we overcompensate by embracing them even more tightly. We cling to old ideas and habits because eliminating familiar (albeit dysfunctional) elements often means treading in the dangerous waters of fear and insecurity. We are really grasping at straws because we want life to be a certain way, but our desperation indicates that we cannot accept that change is the only sure thing in life. Furthermore, we fail to recognize how counterproductive our stubbornness has become. We simply cannot see that life is fluid because we sometimes want everything to stay frozen in place.

As a result, we turn into caricatures of our younger selves and routinely dismiss some rational concepts and suggestions from those around us. Our obstinate nature pushes loved ones away, even when we do not want to alienate them. However, even a complete break from a valued relationship can sometimes seem preferable to dealing with the fears that arise when the need for alterations comes knocking at our door. Fortunately, most of us do rise to the challenges and mellow, but whether we comply or resist when the times demand it, our journey through life is rarely smooth and uneventful, except for those wonderful lulls that we discussed earlier.

Under the best of circumstances, the bumpy road through spiritual evolution is twisted, muddy, and full of opportunities to exit. Some off-ramps take us to resting areas with a multitude of distractions, while others lead straight to self-destruction and potentially ruinous options, such as addiction.

Addiction

Our drive for diversions and panaceas—and to Hell with the consequences—reflects the unconscious. However, we are spiritually obligated to face the music, and if we run for cover in the form of escapist activities, such as addiction, we compound the situation by adding yet another set of unpleasant variables.

In light of this, the dry-drunk syndrome is fascinating to observe and applies to all addictions. The "dry drunk" is someone who gave up alcohol, but has resolved very few of her underlying issues. The dry drunk typically switches venues, replacing alcohol with another addiction, usually something less toxic. However, sometimes the new addiction is just as detrimental as the old. For example, I know one dry drunk who soberly became a compulsive gambler.

As I managed 1,300 calories a day most of the time, I was hopelessly addicted to a computer game and to buying jazz CDs. I had transferred a food addiction to less virulent obsessions. I frittered away a lot of time on these activities instead of getting on with my life, but I stayed away from excess food on most days.

However, I was still addicted. Like the dry drunk, I was not dealing with the underlying issues that catalyzed the eating disorder. Because losing weight was such a medical priority, I forgave myself for the silly distractions and prayed that whatever needed to be faced would reveal itself when I was ready.

As these examples indicate, being a dry drunk can be a good thing if an addiction is replaced by something significantly less damaging. At least the dry drunk has eliminated the complications arising from the more dangerous addiction. For example, an alcoholic who stops drinking abruptly terminates the predictable erosion of her liver and pancreas. Sober alcoholics are also rational 24/7 and stand a much better chance of retaining jobs and relationships.

However, the case of the dry drunk who became an obsessive gambler illustrates that exchanging one addiction for another is not always desirable. It depends on the trade, which has to do with the subject's level of development and conscious awareness. Therefore, our compulsion to substitute one unhealthy behavior for another of equal or greater toxicity underscores our fear of broadening our self-knowledge.

Addiction and Windows of Opportunity

Compared with substances such as alcohol and painkillers—or diet pills and prescription sleep aids—drugs such as methamphetamine, cocaine, and crack offer a much narrower window of opportunity for reversing the physical damage caused by their use.

Our bodies are more vulnerable and less forgiving over time than some of us realize. Doctors are sometimes astounded by a patient's complete reversal of an addiction-induced condition, but most of us do not enjoy such a miracle after we have pushed the envelope too far. Therefore, those of us who wait too long to successfully purge a substance from our system cannot usually overcome the natural laws leading to irreversible conditions.

We are not being punished, nor does this refer to negative karma, as some would tell us. Rather, we are being subjected directly to the consequences of our own actions in the real world. In my case, I got a handle on my eating problem only after I was in a wheelchair. I can prevent more weight from accumulating by taking in just 1,300 calories and following a regime of 30 minutes of sit-down exercises a day, but I will have to reduce my caloric intake much further to accomplish any real weight loss. So far, this has proven to be quite a difficult challenge.

Even so, my medical conditions are now past the point of no return, so the best I can hope for is some reduction in the pain associated with my situation, along with a reduced risk for strokes and heart attacks. This is of great value of course, but it is a far cry from a reversal substantial enough to allow me to walk again. That ship has sailed.

Unlike most people in wheelchairs, I could have prevented my situation had I acted in a timely fashion. I do not blame bad karma. I know I did this to myself and I do not expect God or the law of attraction to rescue me from the hole I have dug.

Lessons Mirrored by a Situation

Some lessons directly reflect the situation itself. For example, a woman may come to understand that she has been attracting similar types of men over and over again to play out the same painful aspects of a romantic relationship. She may have to go through a dozen men to see this clearly because not only do the faces change with each new man, so do the peripheral circumstances.

For example, she might find that all of these men share an aloofness and a refusal to communicate when she most needs to talk. However, each man's life, his personality, and the relationship itself can be so vastly different from the men before him that they mask the essence of the troubling common denominators.

In some cases, these unhealthy features point to an old situation we have failed to excavate from our psyches. In others, they reflect a flaw in our own makeup that needs adjustment. For example, attracting controlling lovers may refer to either recreating a controlling parent or to our own need to control others.

The Insane, the Eccentric, and the Odd

The series of events that led to my awakening were particularly bizarre. For many years, I kept meeting crazy people in the rooming houses in which I lived.

"Crazy" is a relative term, of course, but my own eccentricities actually fell within a socially acceptable framework. However, my housemates were genuinely nonfunctional. They were in and out of mental hospitals with predictable regularity and had truly daunting diagnoses.

For these individuals, inappropriate behavior was the norm. One of them even squatted over a trash can in the living room to pee in front of people—when the bathroom was *unoccupied.*

Another roommate taped a long, incoherent note to my door featuring a vivid drawing of a chubby duck hanging from a gallows adjacent to a yet-to-be-used guillotine platform. Then a thick black marker etched a substitute for her signature. The note concluded with: "Whack, Whack!!!"

Yet another roommate once asked me what medications I was taking. When I told him the name of my anti-inflammatory, his disappointment was palpable. He stared forlornly at his own collection of a dozen or more pill bottles, almost all of which contained either anti-psychotics or medications for offsetting the side effects of anti-psychotics.

When I was able to upgrade to an efficiency apartment, my new landlady turned out to be every bit as distressing as the people I had just left. She claimed to have a diagnosed borderline-personality disorder, but she exhibited all the symptoms of something more serious. At the drop of a hat, she would announce, "You are *so* evicted!" In one case, she ranted and raved because I waited a week to tell her that the faucet needed a new washer. Only a copy of my lease and a reminder that my rent had been paid in full could quell these outbursts for a little while.

Finally, she put the house up for sale. One day, with no provocation whatsoever, she screamed at a potential buyer over the phone, "How *dare you* send a roof inspector out at midnight. That's it, the deal's off!" Bang. Dial tone. Not only do roofers recoil from inspections after sunset, but this accusation also came a week *before* the interested buyers had booked a roof inspector.

After years of this, I slowly came to understand what I had in common with these people. My unconventional behavior could not hold a candle to their raving lunacy, but when I realized that "crazy" almost always means "irrational," I finally got it. It took me a long time to understand that exaggeration routinely figures into the learning of life lessons. I was not supposed to learn that I was crazy, but rather that a form of absurdity adversely affected one or more areas of my life. I did not comprehend the specifics until much later, but I eventually understood in hindsight how unwittingly prescient these characters had been.

During this awful period, I was also besieged on another front. I had many sick cars, with ailments ranging from stage-four transmission-oma to inoperable head gasket-itis. I drove one lemon after another into the ground. I had such bad luck that a friend said he wanted my opinion while he shopped for cars. He would ask me which ones I liked so he could focus on the others.

Eventually, I was able to connect the cars and the crazies to my pathological resistance to losing weight, which had become my undoing. Mentally stable people and reliable vehicles returned to my life when I recognized this truth, but the understanding came too late to reverse my physical deterioration. The Universe had been telling me how insane I was to maintain a high weight long before three herniated disks deteriorated into incurable conditions. My ludicrous outer world had been mirroring the irrationality of my inner life.

Once I fathomed the enormous consequences of my failure to act, I had no choice but to accept responsibility for my own downfall. Coming to terms with this was extremely difficult, but it turned out to be an early indication of spiritual maturity. Learning that we sometimes design our own demise is one of the most important things we must comprehend. As I found out the hard way, detecting these facets can be extremely difficult even when we are willing to do so.

Not all adverse circumstances directly reflect core issues like the ones cited above. Some refer to anything but the situation itself. For example, if faulty gas lines ignite a fire that seriously damages our home, we cannot be expected to connect the damage to our spiritual development. These seemingly random events are much harder to analyze in a way that yields quick and clear insights.

I know first hand that it can take forever for repetitive patterns to generate a critical realization. I now believe that certain events defy a satisfactory interpretation. In essence, the underlying spiritual factors may be unknowable because the Universe most certainly embodies elusive mysteries.

In any case, those blessed (or cursed) with an analytical mind and a sincere interest in spiritual advancement undergo the most frustration in interpreting a given situation, such as the house fire. We simply do not get it and, frankly, we do not need to. Our task is to make the best of whatever cards we have been dealt. Furthermore, if a given situation calls for sacrifice, we must decide whether or not we are up to that kind of demand.

Sacrifice

To a large extent, we can choose the degree of sacrifice in our lives. For example, some college students may select a major based on the amount of sacrifice involved, at least unconsciously. One student may opt for social work because the sacrifice and personal involvement in this career would be far greater than a job within the corporate world. This woman may feel that she wants to "give back to the community." Another student might reject the helping professions because she feels ill prepared for such demands, but she will be presented with opportunities for sacrifice in other ways.

Our personal development does not depend on sacrifices, but forfeitures for the greater good, or those motivated by love, can prove to be great assets both in the scheme of things and in relationship to our karmic standing.

Parental Sacrifice

Parents certainly understand that routinely relinquishing time and resources for the sake of their children goes with the territory of child-rearing. Parents often go on automatic pilot in terms of sacrifice for their kids, but this does not diminish the value of each and every beneficial act. Parental sacrifice is motivated by love and the dream of making a decent life for our children. Hence, everything a parent does to fulfill this vision counts in a major way in the spiritual realm. Sometimes parenthood may seem like a thankless endeavor, but great spiritual strides are being made.

In addition to demanding sacrifices, parenthood also forces us to deal with a given child's personality and behavior. If we are not blessed with a perfect child—and precious few of us are—the resulting conflicts can help us to grow spiritually.

Special-Needs Children

Raising a healthy child can sometimes be a roller coaster ride for even the most loving parents. However, a serious condition detected at birth, such as cerebral palsy, dramatically increases the emotional turmoil. Such a situation will dominate several lives for a very long time. Both the parents and the child can expect a degree of desolation that other families never face. Misery is always there and it never goes away. However, amidst the sorrow, these families often find illumination and great joy, as we shall see later on.

Parents of a special-needs child find that their lives now revolve around the child's condition and the degree of sacrifice goes way beyond what would have been the case with a healthy child. Early on, each parent decides on their degree of commitment, which in turn determines their level of sacrifice.

For his part, the child understands in due course how different he is from his peers. This recognition usually contrasts with how he feels inside. He desires involvement with kids his own age, but he is physically incapable of engaging in typical activities.

This theme may change forms as he gets older, but his sense of deprivation and longing usually worsen over time. His many challenges include coming to terms with the many unusual and heart-wrenching facets of his situation.

Even in the most loving environment, all parties to this situation have their spiritual work cut out for them. Over time, they eventually see life from a totally different perspective and this may realign their thinking and significantly revise their values and priorities. If they rise to the challenges inherent in this situation, considerable spiritual growth is virtually guaranteed.

We often observe a deep, resonating joy emanating from special-needs children and their parents. The love transmitted among them is sometimes palpable and we easily recognize its exceptional nature. These families have transcended the trivialities that often govern the lives of "normal" families. Ordinary parents love their children as much as parents of a disabled child love theirs. However, the "special" family sometimes *expresses* their love in a seemingly purer form because they have risen above daily distractions to focus on the essence of their relationship, as if the preciousness of life surpasses all other matters.

Voluntary Sacrifice

When we voluntarily sacrifice for the sake of others, we make great strides in the spiritual realm. Our motives are important: If we make sacrifices as partial payment for a ticket to heaven or as a mask for martyrdom, it counts a whole lot less than if we are motivated to help others just because it is the right thing to do. At its highest spiritual octave, sacrifice means being solely inspired by love. Sacrifice and acts of love manifest in many ways, even in a soup kitchen.

The Soup Kitchen

I remember a story on TV about an upscale couple who had clearly undergone a profound spiritual transformation. They worked full-time at their six-figure-income jobs and part-time at a soup kitchen. Eventually, their compassion and an overpowering sense of purpose led them to sell their home and cash out all their assets.

They took the entire sum and donated it to the soup kitchen in exchange for an austere place to live in the rear of the building. Their new home was not much bigger than a prison cell with a double bed and a chest of drawers. Like monks in a monastery, they were dependent on the soup kitchen for basic necessities. The couple said they wanted to devote the rest of their lives to service. Almost everyone they knew thought they were insane.

This story illustrates spiritual grace in action, but it is far more dramatic than anything we need to contemplate for ourselves. We do not have to actively pursue situations that demand such extreme forfeiture on our part. Opportunities for sacrifice ultimately boil down to responding to situations as they arise. At such times, we should ask: If someone is in trouble, can I help? Can I cope with the degree of sacrifice that the situation demands?

If we decide to undertake a selfless endeavor, we must not be hard on ourselves if our motives fall short of pristine at first. For those of us who are unaccustomed to thinking in loving, giving terms, going through such a decision process and following up with a considerate deed is still meaningful. For the uninitiated, completing a loving act is far more important than rising to Saint Teresa's level. Let's leave sainthood to those precious few souls who are near that state anyway.

Our Direction Counts More than the Distance Covered

Spiritually speaking, we achieve a lot when we climb several rungs higher than where we began at birth. This may not sound like much, but when we factor in the people who slide down the ladder, we can see that any movement upwards represents an accomplishment, as if the direction we take is more important than the degree of advancement.

Furthermore, moving up spiritually sometimes encompasses devolving finances, health, etc. Conversely, descending could consist of countless opportunities for worldly advances. We often see examples of the evil inheriting the Earth, but the meek and spiritually attuned souls are bequeathed so much more.

We should also bear in mind that small acts of kindness accrue over time. Furthermore, when we reconfigure our thinking to consciously acknowledge the needs of others, these offers to help start to come naturally and we feel better about ourselves at day's end.

Involuntary Sacrifices Associated with Poverty

One note about sacrifice in my life: I did not have children and really felt no motivation to sacrifice in other areas to any appreciable degree. I was later plagued by lack for so long that these deprivations could have been connected to the sacrifices I should have made but did not. I do not believe this is the only interpretation of the scarcity in my life, but it does seem like one reasonable possibility.

In my poorest days, I sometimes had to decide between groceries and gas, so we could argue that I had to sacrifice one for the other. However, this would be a superficial assessment at best. These kinds of difficult choices dogged me for a very long time, but did not have any spiritual value because they did not affect others. (Of course, I am not counting the dozens of banks and convenience stores I cased, but at the last minute, chickened out and did not rob.) Therefore, my quasi sacrifices could be grouped with all the other adversities: Together they formed a substantial platform for internal transformation. By the time the period of lack ended, I found myself compassionate for the first time and certainly empathetic to the needs of the underprivileged around the globe.

Sacrifice and Wealth

Long-term poverty creates chronic pressures and situations that would all vanish if money were introduced. However, a host of misfortunes can interfere with the well being we associate with the very affluent as well. For example, addiction, a grave medical prognosis, or the loss of a loved one affect all income levels. Therefore, no matter where we stand on the economic scale, we are never exempt from hardships. The variation of misfortunes among us mirrors the countless possible adversities out there.

High-Contrast Choices: The Golden Bridge to Hell

The filthy rich, the middle-class, and the dirt poor share at least two things in common: Decisions. Decisions.

Some situations present excruciating choices, such as choosing between going into debt for dental care and living with the pain of an abscessed wisdom tooth. Other options are no-brainers, or high-contrast choices. Sometimes our opportunities feature one ho-hum possibility versus a spectacular one. For example, do I want to continue living in a dull town, working at a low-paying and inconsequential job, when I can relocate 1,000 miles away for triple the salary doing my dream job?

Monica and Brad

I remember an acquaintance named Monica when she considered just such a scenario. At the time, she had a husband, three children under the age of 10, and two dogs. Monica and her husband, Brad, believed that this offer promised such a financial boost that they could exchange their paycheck-to-paycheck existence for relaxed affluence within the year.

Monica's prospective employer also had a job posting for which Brad qualified, but it offered only a small pay increase compared to Brad's current position. Nevertheless, the couple thought that the whole package—including a 300 percent pay raise for Monica— was irresistible, so Brad applied for the job. Soon enough, this established multi-national company hired both of them. Brad and Monica thought they had hit the jackpot. Everything seemed to fall magically into place to make the required relocation possible. They were able to sell their home for its full market value and they looked forward to enrolling their children in new public schools. These schools ranked high on national test scores and were much better equipped than the ones they were leaving.

Furthermore, in their new location, Brad and Monica would be able to carpool most of the time, saving money on gas. The company also offered free perks such as a 24-hour gym, catered lunches, and daycare for their pre-schooler. Once they passed the three-month probationary period they would even qualify for college tuition reimbursement, performance-based bonuses, and a 70 percent discount on items produced by the company. The benefits just went on and on.

For the most part, their expectations were met by both the new city and their new jobs. Six months later, Brad and Monica were still awash in gratitude for this huge break and they looked forward to many more wonderful years there.

Then it hit the fan. A large scandal rocked the Fortune 100 company. Financial improprieties to the tune of $600 million rolled through like a 9.0 earthquake. Nobody knew what this would ultimately mean, but workers could cut the tension with a knife.

The first visible repercussions involved drastic cutbacks on employee perks: The daycare and the gym would now cost the same as private ones. The catering service was replaced with vending machines. Tuition rebates were eliminated and an immediate hiring freeze was implemented. Within three months, the company's stock shrank to one-third of the all-time high it hit just before the scandal.

Almost every night, Monica and Brad tried to work out a contingency plan in case they were laid off. They searched high and low on the Internet for new jobs, hoping to quit before they were fired. They had very little cash on hand because all of their extra money went towards reducing an enormous credit card debt they never would have accumulated if they had known what was coming.

In the end, they were both part of a mass layoff that was implemented almost to the day of their one-year employment anniversary. This news could not have come at a worse time: Monica found out she was pregnant and Brad had just been diagnosed with treatable colon cancer, but they had now lost their health insurance. Furthermore, the national economy had sunk to its lowest point in eight years, causing workers all across the country to jealously guard their jobs.

The family dealt with one hardship after another for years because they were never able to recover from the blow and its ripple effect. They longed to live paycheck-to-paycheck again because they were now forced to live hand-to-mouth at best.

This scenario plays out with frightening regularity in our culture, though the particulars vary from one situation to another. A seemingly wonderful opportunity may devolve into a golden bridge to Hell. We have no way of identifying these situations in advance, so we usually cannot forecast the horrors that await us.

When we travel over the golden bridge—only to end up in Hell—we feel like lambs ready for slaughter. In some vague way, we may feel betrayed by the promise of a wondrous future. However, these gilded journeys to ruin represent one example of the adage, "Everything happens for a reason," though the reasons are rarely clear.

Petitions to God and the Golden Bridge to Hell

The golden bridge to Hell often results from petitions to God, as author John Randolph Price explains:

> When [we] initially contact the inner realm, [we] have only the amount of creative energy stored in reserve. When [we] tap that energy, it works wonders . . . but at some point the energy [depletes] and [we] once again function on limited resources.
>
> John Randolph Price
> *The Superbeings*

In my own life, feverish recitations of affirmations incited a burst of energy and I incorrectly assumed that I had tapped into a bottomless reservoir. Promoters of the law of attraction never take this phenomenon into account and *The Secret* strongly suggests that this high level will continue, or even rise, as long as we follow *The Secret's* advice.

Princess Diana's Golden Bridge

Perhaps Princess Diana would have said that she, too. crossed a golden bridge to Hell when her whirlwind courtship with Prince Charles transformed into strained relations at the palace, telescopic scrutiny by the paparazzi, a painful divorce, and, finally, her untimely death.

These stories illustrate high-contrast options in decision-making that eventually lead to horrible outcomes. Similarly, low-contrast choices—which translate to the lesser of two evils—also trigger or sustain dark nights of the soul.

Low-Contrast Choices: The Lesser of Two Evils

When one option appears to be nearly as gloomy as the other, a painful decision awaits. During my bleak years, a lack of money prevented me from escaping unpleasant situations and also skidded me into dead ends.

When my money completely dried up in Los Angeles, I was evicted. I had only one offer that would keep me out of the homeless world: Living with a friend at her psychotic mother's home. I knew about this woman's erratic and destructive behavior and presumed I would be a welcome target of her wrath. It turned out to be like that and then some.

I really had no choice but to proceed with the move, no matter how much I dreaded it. Selling my car gave me enough money for a one-way ticket to this carnival of chaos and the means to forward 20 boxes with $100 left over. My only other option was to live out of the car in Los Angeles and lose all of my possessions. Both low-contrast and high-contrast choices steer us in one distinct direction: The place we are meant to be to further our growth at that time.

Everything Happens for a Reason

"Everything happens for a reason" is a popular concept in our culture. I believe that this adage includes the outcomes of both low-contrast and high-contrast decision-making. Likewise, family members and close friends—along with the most irritating and threatening individuals—serve a higher purpose. Nevertheless, several issues challenge this notion in its raw, unqualified form:

One, we sometimes base our choices on poor or ill-informed judgment and such decisions illustrate how free will occasionally bedevils us. More often than not, our lives are quite messy as a result. However, the Universe offers us an endless array of contingencies to offset the consequences of deficient judgment. These backup plans usually contain events and people that "happen for a reason." Therefore, free will permits us to veer from situations containing spiritually charged events and people.

Two, our tenure on Earth consists of a collection of destined and random events. We rarely identify situations as such or even consciously think in these terms, but we go back and forth between destiny and chance all the time.

Three, examining real-world manifestations and those generated by the spiritual world offer illumination: In direct opposition to *The Secret's* principles, we most often rely solely on our own wherewithal to achieve a specific goal. For example, let's look at successful business owners: Among the people I have known over the years who have created viable enterprises, I cannot recall even one who did not work extremely hard and suffer many setbacks along the way, including such serious obstacles that they threatened to abort the whole operation.

These success stories called for persistence, self-reliance, and real-world means. However, help sometimes comes to us unexpectedly when we are lost in a situation and cannot figure out a solution. In these cases, our spirits probably attract this assistance. When we recall such examples from our own observations, these so-called "miracles" are rarely as extraordinary as *The Secret* promises.

Four, not every soul who populates our lives can be viewed as important. For example, when we drive along the freeway our passengers might be spiritually significant, but the other drivers are merely inconsequential bit players for us and we then become extras in their productions.

I am reminded of a monochromatic color scheme with black and white at each end and many shades of gray in between. Let's say that the white represents the most important spiritual events and people in our lives, while the black reflects the most trivial. When we ponder our lives we find that most of the situations and people we encounter fall into the gray spectrum. Therefore, the grays reflect lesser events and persons and "everything happens for a reason" may or may not apply.

Adversity Brings Us Closer to God

Metaphysicians and theologians tell us that God is closest to us when we feel forsaken and lost in suffering. Author Joel Goldsmith talks of plummeting into a state of "disease, lack, or limitation." He says we can be assured that our "sense of separation from God" causes these experiences so we will want to move closer to God's grace. We do not really need to search for God, because God is omnipresent right where we are in the midst of this seeming danger.[20]

Saint Teresa said that we can and "must expect suffering." It is a sign that "Jesus is near." He stands by watching and suffering along with us. "Suffering empties us out for Jesus."[21]

In this chapter, we discussed some real-world difficulties and factors outside ourselves that contribute to our misery. In the next chapter, we will consider internal and self-generated sources of distress.

Chapter 4

The Laws Governing Internal Sources of Suffering

A thin, blurry line separates some psychological theories from spiritual matters. The sheer number of overlaps between psychology/psychiatry and metaphysics astounds me at times. In addition, one camp addresses pertinent issues that can be borrowed by the other for deeper understanding. Fortunately, numerous insightful books, written by psychologists and psychiatrists, have helped in my personal journey as well as my ongoing research.

Psychology, Psychiatry, and Metaphysics

Psychological or psychiatric counseling may serve some people well, particularly those who have yet to awaken spiritually. Successfully applied techniques and talk therapy can be every bit as helpful as confronting real-life issues in a pragmatic fashion.

The goals of therapy patients typically include living richer, fuller lives, which is completely in sync with their spiritual agendas. Furthermore, when we consult a psychiatrist or psychologist, we work from the inside out, as we do with a strictly spiritual approach.

Whether or not we seek professional help, this discussion boils down to our responsiveness at any given time to a particular approach. At certain points, some of us might find a perceptive friend to be enough, while others feel satisfied with a life coach. For deeply rooted issues, we may find that a psychiatrist is our best option. The good news is that we have plenty of choices to suit our ever-evolving consciousnesses and changing needs.

Carl Jung's Prolific Work

References to Swiss psychiatrist Carl Jung (1875-1961) are scattered throughout this book. Of all the psychologists who surfaced in the last century, none had a better grasp on the spiritual aspects of psychology than Jung and the Jungian analysts who subsequently enhanced his material. Jung's writings reveal spiritually attuned perceptions and remarkable, forward thinking. Moreover, Jung's work was clearly influenced by his longstanding interest in mysticism, Christianity, Hinduism, Buddhism, Gnosticism, and Taoism, according to Wikipedia.

In books geared towards the public, the Jungian analysts' contemporary writings usually reflect a clearer and more accessible rendering of Jung's theories than Jung's original work. Jungian analysts have apparently mulled over Jung's writings and have routinely added astonishing perceptions that typically remain faithful to Jung's intentions.

Studies of consciousness and the unconscious dominated Jung's work. He also focused on dream interpretation in a revolutionary way. Jung coined many familiar terms, such as the *shadow, archetypes, synchronicity, extravert/introvert,* and the *collective unconscious*. Jung also proposed the *anima/animus* hypothesis, but only half of this equation is vaguely conveyed today when we talk about a man's "feminine side."

Alice Miller and Childhood Issues

Jung often discussed the nuances of family dysfunction that can lead to an existential handicap in adulthood, but Swiss psychologist Alice Miller (1923-) devoted most of her professional life to this subject. (Strangely enough, after decades working as a psychoanalyst, Miller ultimately rejected psychoanalysis as a viable treatment option in 1988, according to

Wikipedia.)

The bulk of this chapter echoes Miller's theories, particularly those found in *The Drama of the Gifted Child* and I am indebted to Miller for introducing these concepts. Comparing the pertinent sections of *The Drama of the Gifted Child* to what I have written reveals Miller's theories to be the scaffolding from which I have built my own theoretical structure.

Supplementary research accounts for some of what follows, but Miller's theories profoundly resonated with my own experiences in an ultra-repressive environment. Consequently, I incorporated Miller's ideas into my own work in a way that will not necessarily be instantly apparent to readers of *The Drama of the Gifted Child.*

Beyond Miller and Jung, I am very grateful to all the psychologists and psychiatrists who have written the books that inspired me in a meaningful way. These authors performed a delicate balancing act: They avoided scientific jargon, preserved the subject's complexity, and refused to dumb down the material.

Submerged Truths

In the last chapter, we completed a lengthy discussion of the concrete troubles that can besiege us from time to time. Even harder to identify and readjust are the hidden aspects of our inner lives, shrouded as they are behind the numerous shielding mechanisms of our unconscious. These protective curtains may as well be thick iron walls, because we cannot see beyond them until such time as our unconscious receives a clear indication from our conscious self that we are now prepared to examine the contents.

Don't Mess with Me

Most of the time, the unconscious resides quietly in our brain and operates on the premise that "if you don't disturb me, I won't mess with you."

Though we rarely notice it most of the time, our unconscious contains a staggering power that both helps and hinders us. It immunizes us from painful events we are not ready to confront and blinds us to traits we are unwilling to acknowledge. Nevertheless, these concealed truths really need to be released and harboring them creates an unnecessary burden that pulls us down.

According to author Robert Bly, we store lots of emotional garbage—usually accumulated in childhood—in an invisible bag that we drag behind us. As adults, our spiritual duty is to empty the bag, one piece at a time.[22] In part, these counterproductive elements consist of:

- Psychological injuries and indignities
- Moments of profound shame
- Instances of abuse or neglect
- Huge losses, such as the death of a parent.

The actual traumatic event or situation is often far less damaging than is our inability to release it. We may not know how to purge something from our system, but the longer we warehouse it, the more distorted our psyche becomes. Consequently, healthy functioning in certain areas can be reduced to the realm of wishful thinking. For example, a sexually abused child may never enjoy a long-term and mutually gratifying relationship as an adult because either her trust in men was destroyed or she cannot overcome the shame she now associates with sex.

Introjects

This instance of shame induced in childhood illustrates "introjects," a term used by Alice Miller in *The Drama of the Gifted Child.* Introjection loosely refers to adopting the characteristics imposed upon us by others. These counterfeit traits result in submerging important aspects of our true selves.[23]

For example, my mother saw me as a "sad sack," and she constantly insisted on smiles, however fake they may have been. I introjected this expectation by stretching my lips in her presence, but I reverted to a neutral expression the rest of the time.

As we see here, elements of my real self were temporarily supplanted by my mother's demand to smile, but this particular introject did not carry over into adulthood because its effects were quite shallow. Superficial and annoying introjects rarely cause permanent, penetrating damage, but others may result in much more debilitating after-effects.

Invisible Vaccines

When parents detect unwanted characteristics in a child, they typically inoculate the child with introjects as an antidote. Some of these behaviors may be universally disdained, such as regular temper tantrums in a child old enough to know better. However, parents who favor introjects as their *modus operandi* often just want to wipe out traits that are inconsistent with *their* agenda for the child. They often do so with no regard for who the child really is and replace the unwanted traits with characteristics the parents find more palatable. In these cases, subjectivity motivates the parent. For example, one parent might see an opinionated child as headstrong and obnoxious while another might view her as lively and assertive, with a bright future ahead of her.

This particular example also calls attention to personality compatibility issues. When parents feel attuned to a child's personality, they are less likely to impose introjects. As a result, parents who are prone to introjecting may do so more with one child than another. In some cases, the introjecting parent's narrow context reflects a set of constrictive and often outdated values relative to the collective consciousness surrounding the parent.

Parenting Trends

Parenting trends sometimes underscore these phenomena. For instance, most of us now recognize the negative, long-term consequences of constantly berating a child. However, now that this is acknowledged, some would say that the pendulum has swung too far in the other direction, with some parents' gushing admiration for a 10-year-old who simply remembers to bring home his lunch bucket. Hopefully, we will eventually achieve a balance between these two extremes by reserving praise for more significant accomplishments.

Here we see signposts of three levels of developing consciousness: In the past, demoralization was common. Today we have over-compensated, leaving our children poorly prepared for the real world. In the future, we will undoubtedly pull back and achieve the balance we sought in the first place.

These three states represent snapshots of different periods of a collective consciousness within a specific culture. (We can take a step further and observe the pendulum at work on a large scale by charting the course of many aspects of a particular culture, from standards for political correctness to sexual mores.)

The Toxicity of Introjects

Now that we have discussed various trends, we will return to introjects. Both the parent (introjector) and the child (introjectee) are susceptible to a highly unconscious process. The parent can neither identify nor forecast the potential toxicity of introjects. For her part, the child innocently ingests them as effortlessly as inhaling carbon monoxide, which is also odorless, tasteless, and virtually impossible to detect. Neither side foresees the existential incarceration awaiting the child in adulthood. Adult introjectees know all too well how punitive invisible imprisonment can be.

By their very nature, introjects are submerged in the realm of the irrational, yet highly functioning adult introjectees often comprehend the full extent of the damage done by introjects. Nevertheless, they can still be utterly immobilized when they contemplate bridging the gap between intellectual understanding and actually releasing themselves from this straightjacket. Introjectees fully understand that such paralysis saturates the psyche to the point that rational thought is all but swallowed up by the introjects.

The Victor, the Vanquished, and the War Within

Once introjects linger long enough to be systemically encoded, the adult introjectee reaches an uneasy impasse. Instead of new thinking unseating the old, our true nature struggles helplessly to free itself from the weight of long-established introjects. Nevertheless, time and again the prevailing introject successfully annihilates all attempts to liberate the real self. These exertions exhaust us until we have stopped fighting and until enough time has passed to reinvigorate our psyche. Then another battle ensues and the introject usually reigns supreme while the true self feebly concedes defeat once again.

Even so, the screams for release continue, but they tend to grow progressively fainter because our authentic disposition plummets deeper into the abyss with each setback. The victor (our introject-command coordinator) confidently settles in for the long haul, while the vanquished (our conscious self) mourns the loss of both our hearty voice and most ambitious wishes. This war within corresponds to a lesser-known interpretation of an old adage: "We truly are our own worst enemies."

Projection

We can understand introjection better when we look at its opposite: Projection, or the assignment of favorable characteristics we wish another person possessed. Projection typically occurs early in a close relationship and can often lead to its demise.

For example, when we are in the initial, giddy stage of a romance, we believe that our partner displays all kinds of idyllic qualities, which amplify our attraction all the more. Within a month or so, we painfully watch as the fictional features disintegrate one by one, exposing the person's true nature, blemishes and all. At this point, the shortcomings shift to the forefront in excruciating contrast to the first idealized image, which we believed was so real just a short time ago.

Eventually, maturity and experience usually armor us against this romantic pitfall, but almost all of us project at one time or another.

Therefore, it is truly miraculous when a relationship survives past this reality check. In romance, projection usually entails casting ideal attributes onto another.

However, we can also transfer shadowy elements within our own psyches onto others. For example, a chronic braggart may grumble about someone else's momentary boasting. In this instance, a third party might make the ironic correlation between the complainant and the accused, but the braggart will remain clueless about the connection.

The essential difference between introjection and projection is their source: Projection generates from within the self, while outside parties typically initiate introjects that we then unwittingly nurture.

Harmless Introjects

Since introjects usually take root in childhood, we need to return to an earlier stage of life to examine them more fully.

Let's look at an innocuous introject in a five-year-old who mimics his father. The child may be pleased that his mother bought him a three-piece suit because he can look more like his dad going off to work every day. In this case, a benign introject is manufactured solely by the child. The boy secretly wants the suit so he can resemble his dad, as opposed to the father insisting that his son wear a suit to maintain family status or impress the neighbors. This last scenario compounded by many other similar parental messages, may lead to a mildly detrimental introject. However, we are more concerned with the kind that lingers into adulthood and messes up our thinking—and sometimes our lives—in a major way.

Malignant Introjects

Injurious introjects can also be created by the introjectee, but they are usually a response to tacit appeals from others. Parents often solicit desired behavior via unvoiced "parental directives."[24] The introjectee understands that much is at stake if she rebuffs the demand and she clearly sees that compliance leads to approval. So the introjectee conforms in classic Pavlovian fashion, regardless of how much of her real self must be sacrificed.

For example, when a child is "caught" exploring her body, a parent may verbally reprimand her or implicitly invoke shame. Either way, the child believes she has done something hideous. This one incident may be all that is needed for the child to conceive a crippling introject that could generate a lifetime of sexual dysfunction.

In *The Drama of the Gifted Child*, Alice Miller exhaustively explores the ramifications in later life of childhood acquiescence to noxious introjects. Miller asserts that the child's obedience to parental mandates—offering shame as punishment and approval as reward—surely instills a sense of conditional love. Furthermore, these dictates may very well work against the child's natural temperament and personality, forcing the child to develop a false identity to satisfy the parent and circumvent degradation. Here, the unspoken message is clear and damaging: Your authentic self is reprehensible and unworthy of our love. Only your counterfeit self—or who you pretend to be to please us—is the one we really love.[25]

As we shall see later in this chapter, the adult introjectee usually chooses between two dysfunctional options: People pleasing and rebellion. Each of these comes with its own can of worms. The deeper the introject's roots, the less likely that healthier options will manifest in that area.

Retroactive Introjects

A retroactive introject can cut as deeply as any other. Retroactive introjects indicate directives that are planted early in life, but only kick in as introjects later.

For example, let's consider a gay man named Blake. For all of his life, Blake heard "faggots" and "queers" being ridiculed, only to find himself attracted to boys when he reached puberty. He then connected what he had heard to this new realization and retroactively introjected all the associated shame. Consequently, Blake only "came out" at 31.

Some gay people never honor who they really are, presumably because retroactive introjects not only overtake their psyche, but also continue to grow in the adult mind. Another introjectee named Heather understands this well, but her situation is quite different.

Early Onset Introjects

The most damaging introjects are formulated before we are teenagers and some of us begin absorbing parental messages at birth.

Because of her lifelong sickly relationship with her mother, Heather came to believe that introjects can begin at birth or even during pregnancy. Heather's mother, Bitsy, made it crystal clear from the beginning that Heather's sole purpose in life was to take care of Bitsy. Forever. This was never stated directly, but Bitsy's expertise in sly manipulation and pronounced learned helplessness were daily mute reminders that Heather was never expected to lead a life of her own.

To complicate matters further, Bitsy transferred an appalling assortment of fears to her daughter, making the child feel that the only safe place in the world was at home with Bitsy. Agoraphobia and numerous other magnified worries virtually imprisoned Heather as an adult and pinned her to Bitsy's territory. At 45, Heather said that her situation had created an invisible umbilical cord that still tied her to Bitsy. The older Heather became, the more her mother deteriorated and the more cunningly she dictated, as if Bitsy had to continually up the ante to ensure her daughter's ongoing "commitment."

By the time Bitsy died, Heather had become a recluse, incapable of truly functioning in the outside world. Her youthful forays into self-reliance had long ago been sabotaged and abandoned, along with a once impressive career. In spite of her outstanding talent and intelligence, Heather remained trapped in the web Bitsy had woven for her. Tragically, Heather died quite prematurely, before she could shake off Bitsy's influence and resume what had once been a full and creative life.

This example illustrates how leftover childhood introjects can seriously inhibit or even disable an otherwise functioning adult. Heather never had the chance to heal because Bitsy persistently fortified Heather's engulfing phobias—fears that Bitsy had implanted in the first place. This in turn paralyzed Heather, who stayed frozen in place, exactly where Bitsy wanted her to be. Heather's story also shows us how a parent's sick influence can survive unabated after the parent's death.

Rebellion and Introjects

Theoretically, Heather could have rebelled, but dissension poses its own set of sticky issues. Mutiny can result in a fresh but equally undesirable situation, such as the one I devised by staying fat to defy my mother's dictates.

I unconsciously believed that the men my mother had targeted would not desire me, which would keep me from getting swept into her fantasy. The trouble was, my weight concealed who I was from those I *wanted* in my life. My appearance formed a satisfactory barricade against sanctioned suitors, but it also sent out the wrong signals to all others. Nevertheless, I kept gaining weight because I was focused solely on *not* living out my mother's dreams. I never realized what a high price I would pay for such insubordination.

Defiance sometimes seems like the answer, but we still end up creating a false self. Rebellion only goes against a given demand, but almost certainly transforms us into something other than who we really are. Whether we conform or dissent, introjectees are typically clueless about long-term consequences.

Heartbreaking Insights

The adult introjectee carries around a lot of unwanted baggage and sad realizations:

- She must acknowledge that she never received her birthright: The unconditional love of her parents
- Because her authentic self was never good enough in her parents'

eyes, she still feels that to be herself is substandard and unworthy of another's love. Consequently, she has a fear of being true to herself because that carries the threat of withdrawn—or never offered—love and approval

- The conforming introjectee risks becoming a chronic people-pleaser, always putting others' needs ahead of her own, even when this is clearly ill-advised
- The rebel may find that she uses disobedience to resist all sorts of unwanted demands and may summon unintended, harmful consequences.

The Disenfranchised

Introjects often grow like an undiagnosed tumor, becoming far larger and more debilitating in adulthood than when first cultivated in childhood. An introjectee's potentially inappropriate reactions can foster a vague sense of disenfranchisement and may prove to be lethal for relationships, careers, and other goals. Furthermore, when introjects rule the unconscious, the introjectee might find life to be limited and stifled. Worst of all, the introjectee has no experience with being all she can be, and that frightening proposition might scare her back into either the conformist or rebellious mode.

It should be clear by now that the contrast between knowing who we really are and slavish obedience to introjects causes anguish and sometimes debilitation. This reminds me of people in wheelchairs facing barriers imposed by inaccessible buildings and roads. The wheelchair-bound can have a life, but not nearly the freedom and flexibility afforded the mobile. In much the same way, sustaining introjects drastically narrows our potential scope.

Mute Commands

Parental directives that trigger introjects are sometimes verbal, but it is the silent, insidious variety that grows the gnarliest roots in the introjectee's psyche. A shame-inducing stare or disapproving glance is quite sufficient to redirect us whenever we deviate from a parent's prescribed course.

Such stealthy cues can be far more powerful than yelling. When a parent verbalizes a point, the child at least has the chance to rebut. However, some households—like the one I grew up in—reserve words for the most banal aspects of living, such as "dinner's ready" or "the car needs a tune-up." Control and mind-shaping are achieved in queasy silence.

The Whispering of the Walls

Susanne Short writes brilliantly on this topic in "The Whispering of the Walls," part of an anthology called *Reclaiming the Inner Child.* [26] Short's quote from Jung vividly sums up both her article and this topic:

> These…things…hang in the air and are vaguely felt by the child, the oppressive atmosphere of foreboding, that seeps into the child's soul like a poisonous vapor…through the thickest walls of silence, through the whitened sepulcher of deceit, complacency, and evasion.
>
> Carl Jung
> *The Development of Personality*

Gulping Down Introjects

We cannot easily challenge the kind of silence that generates such distress. In my case, growing up this way meant that I got a daily dose of "I can't accept you the way you are," in one form or another. I found myself at a loss to respond and simply gulped it down.

Other oppressive elements consisted of my mother's concerted efforts to mold me into a clone of herself, including imposing her values on my education and, later, on my choices in men. The local schools with the highest standards included one Catholic university and two religiously diverse ones. My mother was constantly pressuring me to marry someone who not only attended the Catholic university, but who also lived within a 30-block radius of my home. In her mind, these criteria were sure to produce the best possible husband for me.

She believed that this combination would translate into what she considered the ideal circumstances for a successful marriage. When I was still unmarried at 25, she panicked and said, "OK, OK, you can marry someone within a 60-block radius." I never told her that I had retired from Catholicism at 14. I knew she would hit the ceiling because her brother was a Jesuit priest and her sister a Sacred Heart nun.

My mother's dreams for my future were completely at odds with both my own plans and my taste in people. I also understood very early that I never wanted children. I thought that I might never marry, or at least not in my 20s and 30s when most men factor in children. My mother's relentless pressure in this area acted as a screwy incentive for me to maintain a high weight. A very insightful person once suggested that my childhood obesity could have been my silent way of asking, "Now can you see who I really am?" Evidently, I continually contrived to become ever bigger than before, irrationally concluding that more of me would be harder to miss. (This discussion represents one version of a reptilian stronghold in a single area.)

Strident Values Clash with Progressive Thinkers

My mother's discordant ideals were shoved down my throat against my will, although I could not see this happening at the time. All I knew was that my mother and I lived in two different worlds and I wanted no part of hers. Over time, my mother's persistence transformed into deeply ingrained introjects.

My mother's narrow consciousness accurately reflected her own dysfunctional upbringing and personal level of spiritual development. Nevertheless, as misguided as she was, my mother was always motivated by love, not malice. Therefore, benign dysfunction simultaneously constitutes several elements related to introjection in spiritual terms:

First, the introjector typically believes she is doing the very best for her child.

Second, the introjector's innermost motives and degree of spiritual evolution determine the extent of her accountability and its impact on her karmic standing. A relatively innocent and spiritually underdeveloped person is far less liable than her more aware and ill-intentioned counterpart.

Third, despite the amount of hazardous waste produced by the introject, the adult introjectee must still accept responsibility. Her time is more wisely spent on efforts to purge the garbage, instead of blaming the introjector, which is a complete waste of energy.

In part, this discussion of introjects stands in for a whole host of unconscious elements that prevent us from satisfying our potential. The more unconscious material we harbor, the more impaired we are when we take steps toward our life goals. Some of us have been so profoundly injured by the magnitude of these unconscious obstructions that we cannot fulfill some of our sacred purposes.

Introjects and Our Spiritual Agendas

Of course, we do not always identify certain opportunities as chances to manifest our spiritual agendas. As a result, we do not recognize that these situations are infused with meaning. Therefore, we do not always accomplish each and every assigned purpose.

In my case, had parenthood been my purpose, I blew it when I had a tubal ligation at 32. To this day, I believe I would have made the world's worst parent. Some people think I was wise to avoid motherhood because I saved an innocent from all the dysfunctions that go along with my reluctance to take responsibility for a child. I believe this to be true and I am very grateful I never became pregnant. If parenthood was the main event and I missed it, then I trust I was also given many other tasks over the years.

Since wastefulness is strongly discouraged in the spiritual world, I believe we have all kinds of contingencies lined up to compensate for our intermittent failures to step up to the plate at the right time. I also believe that failing at one purpose does not interfere with our karmic standing.

Instead, missing these occasions merely postpones unique opportunities for either learning or serving.

Dreams

Within the unconscious we also house dreams that kick in during sleep to deliver messages through visual metaphors. However, our memories of dreams do not usually last long after we wake up because of the sudden shift in orientation. Our conscious mind springs back into alertness while our unconscious hastily retreats. Our dream memories then assimilate into the unconscious, where they join a large inventory of previous dreams.

Recurring Dreams

Certain dreams re-emerge from our mental vault on a regular basis because a particular dream message was not understood the first time around.

For example, I used to repeatedly dream about flying over escalators and stairs. I was always pleased that I was getting somewhere faster than everyone else, using a method they had not thought of. This dream was repeated dozens of times while I was in the throes of multiple affirmations and the dreams stopped once I understood that floating over stairs really meant that I was skipping steps.

When we are lucky enough to remember a dream, we are often at a loss to decipher it. However, dream interpretation can be a very useful resource, especially during difficult times. It is always a good idea to write the dream down as quickly as possible. Then we can consult a dream dictionary for help in decoding the imagery.

Time and again, Sandra Thomson's *Cloud Nine: A Dreamer's Dictionary* has shed valuable light on my dreams. Thomson's influences are primarily Jungian but they also seem sharply intuitive. Valuable search tips are located at the beginning of *Cloud Nine,* and the main things to pinpoint are obvious symbols. For example, the icons might be stairs and escalators, as in the dream described above. One can also search for actions, such as falling and running. In addition, several entries in

Cloud Nine show numerous and unexpected meanings for a symbol, such as snakes.

Although the process of dream interpretation is a bit of an imposition, the rewards can be priceless. We can comprehend important themes faster when we take the hints than when we ignore dreams. Moreover, the inconvenience of recording dreams is less painful than maintaining aggravating people and situations in our lives. Of course, successful dream analysis neither pre-empts day-to-day malaise, nor does it instantly resolve nasty circumstances. However, it can provide a useful, and sometimes powerful tool for greater awareness.

Unconscious Obstacles

Whether or not we use dreams to deepen our comprehension of our spirit and psyche, we must still deal with the disparities between our conscious and unconscious selves. A strong barrier exists in our waking lives between these factors. As previously discussed, the unconscious protects us from memories and revelations that we cannot handle if they are brought to consciousness. However, the gap between awareness and the unconscious causes odd and unexpected choices in our lives.

Clotaire Rapaille's reptilian-brain theory (introduced in Chapter 2) fits in well with our discussion of unconscious obstacles because the material we allow the unconscious to protect obstructs our ability to reason to one extent or another. Moreover, the garbage that we need to expunge often arises during our impressionable preschool period, when the reptilian brain dominates. Fortunately, the rifts between our intellect and unconscious are almost always confined to one or two areas of our lives. If this were not the case, we would see far fewer fully functioning adults.

Denial

Denial is temporarily housed in the unconscious. Sometimes, we cannot face certain realities, so we refuse to acknowledge them. For example, a

20-year-old man may tell his parents that he has signed up for the military and is shipping out to Iraq, three months after basic training. One parent may either accept this or scream and yell. The other parent may find the news so overwhelming that he can only shut down and refuse to acknowledge it. The fear of what may await his son in Iraq makes him deny the upcoming deployment, at least temporarily.

Denial's length of stay varies according to what is being staved off and how threatening its revelation would be. We may stay in denial about the death of a loved one for several days leading up to the funeral, when reality finally sinks in. This kind of denial can be very beneficial because mourners need time to process their loss.

However, we can also permanently store traumatic childhood events in the unconscious and never allow them to surface. The unconscious often conceals things that could lead to realizations that are important for spiritual development. For example, we sometimes comprehend that it would be too painful to own up to a shadow characteristic or to our participation in a traumatic event. In these instances, the unconscious shields us from the information until we are ready for its revelation. This block is in effect from the moment we plant something in our unconscious in its embryonic form. Our spirit usually makes no demands on us to dig up these items until later in life, but the counterproductive effects of submerging such events or characteristics begin as soon as we store them, and their toxins and tentacles multiply over time.

For some of us, the knowledge never surfaces because we constantly fight the process. Others can only handle a little knowledge at a time, leading to Jung's assessment of "the mellowing of the personality" over the years. The more ambitious among us pray for these awakenings and attract a substantial number of irksome people and troubling situations to trigger the necessary realizations. Yes, the law of attraction thrives, but this is one of very few ways in which it manifests itself in a meaningful fashion.[27]

Remember: We would not be on Earth if we had everything worked out perfectly. Therefore, each of us has counterproductive stuff in our unconscious and our words and behaviors reflect this to one degree or another.

Most of us have visible or subtle neuroses that inferentially expose unconscious elements. However, we may not recognize that another person's neurotic bent is matched by a similar leaning on our part. When we say "like attracts like," we mean that we tend to pursue those who have comparable spiritual compositions. As a result, we unconsciously befriend those similar to us. For example, a slightly dysfunctional person may associate with others like herself. Similarly, a person whose life is too hectic to afford inward reflection might attract other busy people most of the time.

Regardless of the unconscious underpinnings, we also find shared values and experiences to be important. No matter what the level of their spiritual development, couples often say that what they have in common accounts for their sustained mutual attraction.

When we talk about "opposites attracting," we refer to our interest in those who possess qualities we wish we had. A common example would be an extravert coupled with an introvert, as Jung writes about extensively. Each party unconsciously knows that somewhere between these opposites lies balance, and the hope that what we lack—but recognize in great abundance in our partner—will rub off on us by association.

Repression

Let's now examine the ramifications of repression, which is defined as:

> The [classic] defense mechanism that protects us from [anxiety-inducing] impulses or ideas by preventing them from becoming conscious.
>
> http://www.dictionary.com

We typically submerge events or characteristics into the unconscious either because they cause more pain than we feel we can handle or because we believe that exposing these elements means facing some kind of penalty, such as harsh disapproval. In some cases, this results in deep depression.

> Wikipedia lists Joseph Schildkraut in 1965 as an early researcher who identified low levels of norepinephrine as the source of severe depression. Later researchers pinpointed serotonin deficiencies. More recent research isolates mechanical breakdowns, such as changes in neurotransmitter production, transmission, re-uptake, and neural sensitivity. Environmental factors are now being considered as significant contributing factors.[28]

Depression and Six Symptoms of Severe Repression

Between my own observations and decades of living under the weight of repression, I have isolated six symptoms that characterize severe repression:

The first incorporates certain instances of clinical depression, as outlined in the previous sidebar. Despite brain chemistry imbalances and neurotransmitter malfunctions, many psychologists believe that depression also reflects a tremendous resistance to concealed emotions. By burying specific experiences and revelations, some of us obstruct lucid realizations that stay submerged beneath our consciousness.

The second symptom of repression points to a relentless need for escape, including:

- A persistent addiction, even if the addict appears to be fully functioning
- A fixation with extreme sports, such as bungee jumping and skydiving. These death-defying activities give such an adrenalin rush that they can be every bit as compelling as cocaine or whiskey. Of course, we refer here to obsessive participation only

- Any other escapist activity that is pursued so excessively that it begs the question: "What am I running away from?"

The third indicator highlights changes for the worse in appearance, as long as this deterioration cannot be traced back to long-term substance abuse, serious injury, or illness. When we check out pictures from when we were in our 20s and 30s, have we aged gracefully (without cosmetic enhancements), or are we barely recognizable? If the latter, then our ongoing battle to prevent unconscious material from reaching consciousness may be the culprit.

The fourth sign of repression encompasses speech and behavior that prompt others to say either, “She doesn’t have a clue,” or, “He’s so out of it, it’s unbelievable.”

The fifth symptom pertains to habitual judging of others. Judging causes all of our energy to be directed towards others and thus distracts us from self-examination.

The final symptom refers to playing the blame game. Those of us who refuse to take responsibility often resort to blaming others as an unconscious diversionary tactic. Blaming others means looking outside of the self for answers, while the real solution lies in delving inwards. Preferring to shift most of the responsibility onto others allows us to dodge accountability.

Victims and Martyrs

Furthermore, those of us who consistently blame others sometimes become prone to martyrdom, or we develop a victim persona.

The victim’s skewed worldview plays out like this: In everyday exchanges, the victim emphasizes events that happen to them, which are usually (but not always) out of their control. They favor the victim image and typically downplay both positive and neutral occurrences that would offset the impact of the supposed victimization. These people are often viewed as having a negative outlook.

A martyr operates from a different platform. Her goals include eliciting sympathy or inducing guilt through her alleged sacrifices. As we have already discussed, sacrifices—motivated solely by love—resonate spiritually. However, the martyr's sacrifices convert into tools for manipulation instead. Therefore, the martyr puts her spiritual health at risk every time she mentions sacrifices as a means to manipulate.

A common example comes from a mother telling her son: "When I gave birth to you, I was in labor for 75 hours." This particular example does represent martyr-like behavior. However, on its own—with no other similar examples—it usually does not reflect a *pattern* of martyrdom. I have known mothers who used this line repeatedly, but they clearly demonstrated that their other sacrifices were expressions of love, not channels for ongoing manipulation.

Appropriate Assignment of Blame

Now that we have discussed victims and martyrs, let's return to our discussion of blame.

In my experiences with men, I constantly ran into the issue of proportional assignment of blame, particularly when I broke up with someone. Time after time, I would only see the man's shortcomings and bemoan his poor choice of methods in terminating the relationship. I focused solely on these aspects and never acknowledged my own part in the relationship's demise.

Decades later, the dense, mental fog cleared to the point that I could see my part in the relationship's dissolution. Furthermore, the balance then shifted so drastically that the men's failings paled in comparison to my own in some instances.

This example illustrates two points:

One, by the time I could see clearly, I had probably changed enough as a person that these revelations did not hurt much compared to becoming aware a lot earlier. Therefore, avoiding responsibility proves to be yet another defense mechanism, residing under the same umbrella as denial.

Two, the blame game in any context wastes precious energy and gets us nowhere, either spiritually or in real life.

The Pain of Repression

The above repression-symptoms list is tricky, because the unconscious does such a good job of protecting us that we may fail to see ourselves in some of these descriptions. People displaying these symptoms usually have no idea of the connections between these behaviors and the repressed emotions buried deep within. Despite the level of existential pain we endure day after day, some of us spend a lifetime unable to make the necessary correlations, even when we receive the midlife "knock at the door."

Given the difficulty of interpreting both toxic people and difficult situations most of the time, should we be concerned with wracking our brains trying to figure all this stuff out? Actually, that is a personal decision. If the issue refers to our prebirth agenda, karma, or purpose, it may accomplish nothing to determine the source of the problem, other than to instill patience as we go through it.

Repression and Mirroring Another's Traits

A discussion of mirroring another's traits would be useful at this point. For example, if I were still cavalier towards others and used one of my landladies as a mirror, I could more quickly understand how others feel when they are subjected to my own thoughtless attitude. If I really grasped this link, then it would be fairly easy to adjust myself.

During trying times, our only real spiritual obligation is to make our way through life as best we can. All the theories presented in this and other books are optional tools. After all, some people read stacks of books and *still* do not get it. They consistently fail to extrapolate the theories and apply them to their own lives. In a similar vein, bypassing books does not prevent us from making pertinent connections within ourselves. Different people need different methods. In my case, books are the answer, though I only gain the best insights years later. For others, an alternative approach would be more suitable. Some people might even require no strategy at all.

"No strategy" probably seems quite odd to readers accustomed to delving deeply into metaphysical material. However, comparing my real-life experiences to what I have read has shown me that the unpleasant people I have met—coupled with the unpalatable situations I have endured—have taught me much more than my entire collection of books.

Reading material comes into play retroactively. As secondary tools, books help me to clarify a past situation more than they illuminate the way forward. I am reminded of a frustrated father telling his teenage daughter, "Wait until *you* have kids; then you'll understand why...." This prediction goes right over a teenager's head and is only understood once she is a mother. Even the best possible guidance can fall on deaf ears until we mature to the point where we can really grasp it.

Caroline Myss Weighs in on Childhood Injuries

Before we leave this topic, I feel compelled to introduce a radically different point of view, particularly in light of two issues: The tenor of this chapter so far and the mindsets of most self-help authors to date.

Author Caroline Myss (pronounced: Mace) has a thought-provoking way of looking at introjects and other massive injuries that we unintentionally fortify. Though some may not agree with Myss, I imagine that other readers' synapses will be all fired up.

Since the mid-1990s, Myss has spent a great deal of energy addressing the debris associated with long-standing wounds. Myss points out that we live in a psychiatrically driven culture, which she believes does more harm than good to our spirit. For example, Myss suggests that we overly accommodate those who carry gaping wounds from major losses or traumatic events that occurred long ago.

After some time has passed, the injured need to heal or they will continue to be imprisoned by the restrictions that accompany the retention of debilitating pain. Unfortunately, our ongoing sympathies serve to keep their anguish alive long past the time when they should have integrated the sorrow into their psyches in a healthy fashion.[29]

When we consider either the subject or her sympathizer, wound-fortification is almost always an unconscious process. The concerned friend simply responds to cultural cues to indulge in the name of sensitivity. The injured party reaps the comforting rewards of such attention, however stifling and regressive the payoffs may be. The outcome proves to be a double-edged sword: This type of attention infuses short-term relief, but the wound's rawness may be significantly extended in time and even magnified in size. Myss invented the term "woundology" to describe this phenomenon.

The Myss Strategy

According to Myss, genuine healing is reached through a different approach, one that allows loved ones to maintain compassion without the coddling. For example, after a suitable grieving period, a caring friend might say, "I can see that you're not over X yet, so please let me know if I can help in any way." This should be the friend's last words on the subject. The onus is then on the other person to solicit help, thereby catapulting these exchanges from her unconscious to her conscious, at least potentially.

We inadvertently revitalize another's wounds by drawing attention to them. Similarly, a grieving person may unconsciously solicit attention by initiating wound-related conversations. To illustrate this, Myss uses the example of a woman whose child had died many years earlier. This woman might say to a coworker, "I passed his room this morning and it all came flooding back." Depending on the listener, the response might range from a few comforting words to giving this woman a free pass for the day so she can squeak by, doing little or no work.[30]

A healthier reaction might include either nodding or saying, "I'm sorry your day started off so poorly," and then changing the subject. However, workplace demands should in no way be compromised by this dialog because working would be far more therapeutic than wallowing.

Therefore, if the grieving woman expects some kind of exemption she will have to ask for it because it will not be offered. Again, this forces her to become conscious of the process and better able to convert her injury into a memory.

Replace Sympathy with Love

As long as outside parties refuse to commiserate, a wound has a chance to shrink eventually to the point of integration. Thus, our compassion should be modified by our concern for the injured person's future. If we understand that clinging to old wounds impairs a person's ability to move upwards and onwards, we can help to speed up the healing process.

If we think about it, we can probably recall a few people whose entire lives revolved around ancient injuries. We can attribute such sorry existences to the manipulations of the sufferer's unconscious, which serve to enhance the wound at the expense of getting on with life. In these cases, we are so busy spinning our wheels that we can frequently miss out on opportunities for joy or advancement in some area.

The Results of Healing Strategies

Too many of us prevent our lives from moving forward after a traumatic incident. Of course, a temporary interruption is not only expected, but also gives the healing process the chance to form its foundation. Years later, however, these potentially therapeutic roots may have shriveled up if the injured person receives constant reinforcement of the trauma. A steadily shrinking wound gives way to the development of curative buds, while a substantial, unprocessed injury surely obstructs the process.

This discussion may seem counterintuitive because talking through an ordeal usually makes more sense. However, once again, timing is everything. Shortly after a trauma, talking can be soothing and restorative, but it does not accomplish anything positive if the wound has festered for a very long time. Rather, digging deep to sever the emotional tethers is the only effective path to liberation.

Rachael's Purging Meditation

My friend Rachael did just that. She had dozens of wounds related to hideous childhood abuses, including repeated instances of incest as well as physical and emotional cruelty. At 45, Rachael decided that she had paid too high a price for carrying this torture around for decades, so she devised a plan. Rachael devoted at least three hours every weekend to a "purging meditation," as she called it. Each session focused on one harrowing incident, which she played out like a movie in her head. If Rachael realized that she had omitted even a small detail, she would "rewind" and start over. Rachael wanted to get right inside that time and place, as if it were actually repeating itself.

With eyes closed, Rachael sat in the Lotus position and watched the re-enactments unfold as she sobbed and wailed. Rachael also relived the attendant physical symptoms, such as a knotted stomach. Whenever Rachael felt the need, she assumed the fetal position and hugged her middle. She cried and shrieked until she was completely spent. Fatigue and total emptiness followed these sessions, sometimes for two days afterwards. In some cases, a single incident required two or three cleansings over several weeks.

The fallout from these marathons pretty much wiped out the rest of the weekend, but Rachael said it was all worth it. At the end of a year or so, she reported a tremendous freedom and "lightness of being." Rachael's life did not improve dramatically, but she had rid herself of all the extra problems associated with maintaining such a substantial load of grief and rage.

Rachael likened her experience to a sober alcoholic's: She could not reverse any previous damage, but she had aborted the relentless degeneration that would have continued had she not intervened. The most noticeable, practical result was the dissolution of mental barricades that had prevented Rachael from having healthy and loving relationships with men.

Rachael would agree with Myss, who proposes that healing refers to shifting from an emotionally laden investment in our wounds to a more detached position. The goal is freedom from the paralyzing ties that bind, without forgetting what happened.[31] Rachael also noticed how vividly we perceive our own traumas compared to the disconnection we feel about the demons that haunt others.

After such intense exercises, we sever the emotional connection to a wound without losing memory of it. Therefore, Rachael's recollections now invoke the same details as before, but she feels little or nothing, as if these horrible events happened to somebody else. Myss describes several instances of this type of mental shift and would probably advise: The sooner we release our traumas and sorrows, the better.

Maintaining such a burden for a long time renders it so familiar that freeing ourselves becomes a frightening proposition. Myss points out that we fear our own untapped power more than we hate dragging around such an enormous weight, even if our spirit has become as disfigured as Quasimoto's spine.

"Doors don't necessarily swing open," Rachael says of her life after healing, "but at least I now have more than enough strength to open them with ease. Also, the sheer number of appealing opportunities has risen dramatically."

Rachael's exercises may seem frightfully ambitious to some and impossible to others. In fact, I would never recommend doing this the way Rachael did. I believe this type of penetrating exercise would be best addressed under the direction of a professional. Rachael had a positive outcome, but I do see this as potentially dangerous for most people, including myself. Instead, we might consider a less dramatic course. One option would be to start small by soliciting daily help from our inner spirit: "Show me the way out of this pain and into a healthier, fuller life."

Oddly enough, using affirmations in this manner—as opposed to asking for material things—can yield positive outcomes in the real world. When we dissolve spiritual hindrances—which sometimes occupy acres of mental real estate—we become more open and receptive to desirable opportunities because purging makes room for them. Therefore, the law of attraction requires free space, or an emptiness of sorts, before it has the remotest chance of working. Despite *The Secret's* one-size-fits-all philosophy, I have yet to meet anyone but Rachael who had created enough vacant space to benefit from *The Secret's* version of the law of attraction in a meaningful fashion.

Check Out Caroline Myss

Readers who are sick and tired of carrying a particular wound may want to check out Myss' books, audios, videos, and calendar of events. Anyone who is truly ready to let go should find Myss to be a powerful guide. Myss' innovative theories undoubtedly propel some people forward for the first time in years.

This chapter illustrates how powerful and disquieting unconscious elements can be. However, when we examine all the factors influencing our spiritual evolution, other aspects emerge, such as the role of our prebirth agenda.

An older soul with a pitiful level of evolution is like the high school thug, slumped in the back row, who tunes out the teacher. All the students are exposed to the same resources, but not everyone takes advantage of them.

Chapter 5

The Laws of Transition—The Prebirth Agenda

Before we dig into the complexities of the prebirth agenda, let's look at the three prevailing beliefs about life after death:

1. We only get one shot and no afterlife awaits us. We are simply buried six feet under and turn into dust
2. We have only one life, but our beliefs and actions while on Earth determine our location in the afterlife. Heaven and Hell would be the potential destinations within the Christian context
3. We are subject to reincarnation, or recurring visits to this plane with time spent in the afterlife between incarnations. The afterlife offers another chance to expand our awareness, to advance spiritually, and to improve our karmic standing.[32]

Between 21 percent and 27 percent of Americans believe specifically in reincarnation.[33] In contrast, a 1999 poll of Americans shows strong beliefs in the afterlife in general as follows:

- Protestants: 86 percent
- Catholics: 83 percent
- Jews: 74 percent
- Adults with no religious affiliation: 58 percent. [34]

Those of us who believe in an afterlife—but who reject reincarnation—may be persuaded that some sort of ethereal period precedes conception. If so, I am convinced that a specific protocol prepares us for our journey. This book implicitly endorses reincarnation theory, but much of what follows could fit in with the other two viewpoints as well.

Consciousness in the Afterlife

After reading and thinking about the prebirth agenda for a very long time, I conclude the following:

When we enter the astral plane after death, we are bewildered by its completely different context. Even after a long illness, we typically cannot be certain that we are actually dead because an elevated sense of confusion temporarily impairs our judgment. A sharp feeling of dislocation and uncertainty are the usual reactions and they only dissipate as we relocate into the upper realms. [35]

Those of us who end up numerous rungs above the entry level may find our stay in the initial locale longer than expected. We may spend a long time in a disoriented state, finding it difficult to either figure out what is going on or to disengage ourselves from the life we just left. How quickly we can adjust to the new environment and how willing we are to let go of earthly matters influence our progress. The higher we go, the more clearly we perceive things and the more comfortable we feel.[36]

After the initial adjustment period, the part of our mind that is connected to our spirit slowly expands to comprehend the astral environment. For those of us with enough moral fiber to have avoided evil acts most of the time, a wonderful place awaits. Most of us like it so much that the pain we experienced while living seems distant, though we can still recall it. Now, in a distress-free context, we begin to understand six basic concepts:

First, we cannot take up permanent residence in the astral plane's peak level until we have made some crucial alterations to our spirit.

Second, we know that returning to Earth is the only way to accomplish such modifications. Indeed, the planet was set up for this purpose alone.

Third, by exercising free will, we can decide the degree of adjustment for our next tenure on Earth. A consultant is assigned to help us create our own plan for the next visit.

Fourth, the specific details of our future life are not revealed to us. Rather, we pick the extent of our discomfort based on our tolerance for pain and on how much material we wish to cover. We choose our new life guided by a scale from one to 100—one being the least painful, while anything over 80 is aggressively discouraged.

Fifth, the overly ambitious may choose a far worse life (to speed up karmic debt payoffs) than those who pace themselves more slowly. For example, the souls who end up in impoverished or war-torn countries might very well have wanted a more rapid return home. However, sometimes those in horrible circumstances have instead agreed to serve a purpose, which also hastens their progress. For example, a person born with a severe birth defect may promote tolerance of people who differ from the mainstream. Perhaps those of us who end up in a more comfortable Western environment understand that the work we have to do will not usually encompass such basic needs as food, shelter, freedom, and safety, but will entail other adversities that better typify the Western experience.

Therefore, in the most general terms, the differences between some people in underdeveloped areas of Bangladesh and affluent Americans refer largely to their respective degree of spiritual drive: The poorest Bangladeshis may want to cram in more opportunities to learn lessons, serve purposes, and pay off karmic arrears than most Americans do.

Sixth, physical comfort is more likely to materialize in Western countries than elsewhere. Nevertheless, we understand that this does not exempt us from our prebirth agenda. Only the forum for our spiritual work differs. Instead of lacking the essentials, we may get a life-threatening disease, lose our house in a tornado, or have to deal with an ongoing hardship, such as taking care of a parent with Alzheimer's for many years while struggling to make a living and support three children. Remember, we do not ask for the disease, the tornado, etc. The agenda is never that specific.

Untapped Wisdom

As mentioned earlier, our mind must expand to take in the after-death experience. The younger we are, the more difficult this is to comprehend. For example, most 18-year-olds believe that they know everything about everything. As we get older, it slowly dawns on us that whatever we actually do know is nothing compared to what we could potentially comprehend. However, this acknowledgement of vast amounts of untapped wisdom still refers exclusively to the knowledge attainable on Earth, without recognizing the cosmic intelligence beyond it.

We see this dichotomy at work every day as we raise our children. For example, most parents are well informed about online predators, but some teenagers react to warnings by keeping their visits to forbidden chat rooms a secret. The child only understands that he is not allowed to do this, without fully grasping the reasoning behind the restriction.

Along the same lines, when a baby starts crawling, parents know they must be ever vigilant. When the parent pulls filthy objects out of the baby's mouth, the child sometimes seems completely mystified by the parent's actions. Clearly, parents utilize a far more expanded consciousness than children do. An adult's sound judgment leads to pre-emptive intervention, but the child rarely comprehends the parent's protective motives.

These examples point out the differences between child and adult consciousnesses to illustrate similar disparities between the adult mind and cosmic intelligence. When the mind slowly expands after death, our awareness eventually permits us to evaluate earthly matters with the same wisdom an adult on Earth possesses relative to a child.

Our maximum level of cosmic comprehension refers solely to our spiritual evolution at the time we die, rather than to our degree of intelligence or to our accumulated knowledge. Therefore, a brilliant woman with multiple graduate degrees does not necessarily fare better than her less educated counterpart in the afterlife. For example, a high school dropout may be far more spiritually evolved than a college professor. True, the teacher carries enough curiosity to continue learning in the afterlife. However, the dropout may still want to learn and may start at a higher level than the teacher. Of course, the path to accumulating afterlife knowledge correlates closely with our level of spiritual determination. Intellectual zeal only gets us so far, while motivation propels us much farther along.

The Afterlife

Whatever our current level of consciousness may be, we can always take time in the afterlife to advance by learning more. This allows us to be better equipped for our upcoming incarnation. However, some souls are anxious to return to Earth because they liked it so much. They skip as many steps as possible and may refuse the opportunity to learn more.

At some point in the afterlife, we also exhibit an understanding that we carry our karmic bank account and unlearned lessons forward into the next incarnation. As pure spiritual entities utilizing a greatly expanded consciousness, we find ourselves well qualified for a new incarnation. At this point, our basic understanding of how our earthly existence relates to our spiritual well being is so vast that all the mysteries and unanswered questions we had on Earth have been addressed in great detail.

Nevertheless, even with this precious knowledge, we sometimes feel wistful. Some of us would prefer to stay in this wonderful place, because we cannot stand the idea that most of the wisdom we have found on this plane will dissolve when we reincarnate on Earth.

Paradoxically, our memory of the afterlife is erased upon conception, but we still retain our level of consciousness, bolstered by what we have learned in the afterlife. We have an altered awareness with no recollection of any afterlife particulars. At conception, our extended afterlife consciousness shrinks to a form suitable for earthly life. Most of us start our new life on a higher spiritual level than we had at the end of our previous incarnation. A newly expanded consciousness informs our behaviors and decisions as we make our way through life. If we continue on the same path, we are virtually guaranteed a more spiritually enriched life, but not necessarily an easier one.

Before we leave the afterlife, most of us want to cling to our enlightened existence, yet we realize that a new life on Earth offers opportunities to attain even greater heights of consciousness. We can lengthen our afterlife tenure by signing up for more studies, but we can only postpone the inevitable for so long. This predicament proves to be a forerunner of the occasionally agonizing decision-making that awaits us on Earth.

Pressure, Stress, and Learning

In the afterlife, we mull over how much pressure we can withstand on Earth while learning a specific lesson and we choose its time of inception. Some of the questions we must consider are:

- Do we want to take a break (maybe for the first time) and opt for a much milder incarnation?
- Conversely, do we want to rev things up because we were disappointed by how little ground we covered in our last incarnation?
- Can we deal with harsh childhood conditions, or do we prefer to wait until adulthood to begin learning lessons?
- Do we allow the process to begin before or after our earthly spiritual awakening.?

In my case, I clearly opted for serious lessons to begin in adulthood and after my spiritual awakening. Before that time, my life seemed to be far more random and it was responsive to my ingenuity. Apparently, I also signed up for a high degree of persistent stress, because I have yet to unearth the unconscious underpinnings that account for maintaining a high weight.

Despite my failure to conquer the root causes of my obesity, I have made tremendous progress in other areas, such as anger management, increased compassion, and a drastically revised attitude. Nevertheless, several unpleasant aspects of my life thrive unabated, such as mystifying, recurring relationship issues and a slow, steady medical decline, to name two. Whenever I think about how much spiritual ground I have covered, I am always astonished by how much work I have left to do.

The Prebirth Agenda Trumps Everything

A long time passed before I understood that my prebirth agenda trumped everything, including the law of attraction, which worked as a weak, subordinate force. I was then able to ascribe to my spiritual blueprint the importance it deserved. In other words, I could finally identify the law of attraction as a feeble factor at best, one that can help with only the most trivial matters.

Once I understood the predominance of my prebirth agenda, I stopped crying foul. I used to see countless people with no greater qualifications than my own succeeding in areas I could only dream of. "Why can't I have this or do that?" I would cry out during the pity parties I threw for myself on a regular basis. I eventually understood that I was responsible for signing a spiritual contract and that it was just too bad if I later found it hard to live with the terms I agreed to. Evidently, I have given the Universe permission to withhold worldly advances until specific lessons have been learned. Clearly, some other people did not check off this particular box on their application forms.

Preparing to Sign the Contract

Before signing anything related to our upcoming incarnation, we need to undergo extensive education. Part of our training includes refresher courses about long-forgotten topics, while the rest embodies new material specifically addressing the advances from our last incarnation. These educational enhancements put everything into fresh perspective. What was a bit foggy before becomes crystal clear.

Finally, we are tested in many different ways to gauge just how well the material has sunk in. If we demonstrate a deep understanding of what we have just absorbed, we move forward to the next phase. If not, refresher courses await us.

Let's now introduce a bit of fiction. The narrative itself may be a flight of the imagination and cannot be taken literally, but we may benefit from pondering the possibilities embedded within it.

Daniel, the Adviser

Following an extensive life review and afterlife education, we have been assigned an adviser, whom I name Daniel for the purposes of this discussion. Armed with a blizzard of paperwork, Daniel's large trolley carries all the pamphlets and books needed for our meeting. Daniel and his associates call the trolley a "crash cart," referring to hospital crash carts, which are also fully stocked with items needed to revive the dead.

Along with application and consent forms, plenty of reading material is at the ready in case some fine points need to be re-explained. Our minds have already stored this material, but resistance to some of the terms and conditions makes us forget from time to time. We don't like everything we have come to understand, so denial sometimes dominates on this ethereal plane, just as it does on Earth. On the flip side, we are blessed with free will here, too, and informed consent is a top priority in the afterlife.

The Application Form

Daniel presents us with an application form, which is used to determine the quality of our new lives. From the earthly plane, we would most certainly opt for the highest possible quality. However, our minds are filled with knowledge unavailable to us on Earth, so it may be a different story. By the time we have passed from our earthly existence, we have endured hardships that we may not be anxious to repeat. Nonetheless, we understand that the fewer return trips we make to Earth, the sooner we can permanently stay in an enlightened state. It is such a dilemma.

Certain features of this system remind me of the Witness Protection program. We cannot dictate the basics, such as:

- Our new location
- Our ethnic/religious orientation
- The circumstances of our upcoming life
- What our parents will be like.

We cannot control these particulars and only our sacred purpose—in conjunction with karmic laws and the level of pressure we choose—will have any influence at all on these variables. We must have faith that whatever awaits us conforms to our current state of evolution and offers the perfect context for further enlightenment.

> Allow me to digress for a moment with a recollection of a *Chicago Hope* (1994-2000) episode. After Alan Burch (Peter McNicholl) dies, he returns in spirit to tell another character about his new incarnation. Alan is now a seven-year-old Bosnian. Even though his dad is an "asshole," his life is not too bad so far. He concludes by saying something to the effect that, "Well, gotta go. I can't be late for my birthday party."
>
> This story illustrates that the unforeseen circumstances of our new life may not be ideal, but could contain several familiar elements, such as birthday parties and disappointing parents. If these features do not directly refer to former incarnations, they most certainly seem typical of the world around us in previous lives. This especially applies to those of us selecting a degree of difficulty similar to the ones we chose in the past.

Of course, some of us may prefer to repeat our most recent incarnation and completely opt out of the improvement program. However, doing so means leaving many factors to chance and a repetition of the kind of life we just left is highly unlikely. Most of us want to sign up for lives filled with opportunities to advance spiritually. The pivotal question is: "To what degree?"

The Chart

Daniel presents us with a chart featuring numbers ranging from one to 100, representing degrees of difficulty in our future life. We are usually limited to choices that fall between 20 and 80. Those who pick a number over 55 must undergo extra counseling, consult the massive library, and write a lengthy paper about why they think they can withstand that degree of pressure. The persuasive power and sincerity of the essay are important considerations, but the judges also need to see many examples of earthly situations that match our chosen position.

Global Considerations

When we think globally, it seems that choosing 55+ is far more popular than we could ever imagine. Evidently, these eager souls want to speed up the process of enlightenment as much as they can.

We need to be mindful that the vast majority of these people usually feel much closer to God than those who opt for a less turbulent stay on Earth. Communion with God is much easier when we are stripped of amenities and basic necessities. The more comfortable we feel, the more likely it is that we will be too distracted to want to communicate with a Higher Power.

We also must not be fooled into thinking that extreme adversities derive from a huge accumulation of past spiritual felonies. An average soul could opt for a rapid karmic payback after lifetimes of taking it easy and slowly incurring more debt. Conversely, others might owe massive amounts from just one incarnation, but they might choose an easy life and rebuff the very notion of karmic reimbursement.

Akashic Records

Therefore, we simply cannot interpret a person's "Akashic" standing by their lot in life. The soul's record-keeping system, Akashic Records log our:

- Karmic transactions
- Lessons learned
- Afterlife education
- Life events
- And much more, as explained by Kevin J. Todeschi in his book about Edgar Cayce:

> Akashic Records, or *The Book of Life*, can be equated to the Universe's super computer system…[which] acts as the central storehouse of all information for every individual who has ever lived upon the Earth…[Today's] vast complex of computer systems and collective databases cannot…come close to the power, the memory, or the omniscient recording capacity of Akashic Records… .
>
> More than just a reservoir of events, Akashic Records contain every deed, word, feeling, thought, and intent that has ever occurred at any time in the history of the world. Much more than simply a memory storehouse, however, these Akashic Records are interactive in that they have a tremendous influence upon our everyday lives, our relationships, our feelings and belief systems, and the potential realities we draw toward us… .
>
> Akashic Records contain the entire history of every soul since the dawn of Creation. These records connect each of us to one another. They contain the stimulus for every archetypal symbol or mythic story, which has ever deeply touched patterns of human behavior and experience. They have been the inspiration for dreams and invention. They draw us toward or repel us from one another. They mold and shape levels of human consciousness…They are the unbiased judge and jury that attempt to guide, educate, and transform every indi-

vidual to become the very best that she or he can be. They embody an ever-changing fluid array of possible futures that are called into potential as we humans interact and learn from the data that has already been accumulated.

Information about these Akashic Records....can be found in folklore, in myth, and throughout the Old and New Testaments. It is traceable at least as far back as the Semitic peoples and includes the Arabs, the Assyrians, the Phoenicians, the Babylonians, and the Hebrews. [Embedded within each of these belief systems is] some kind of celestial tablet...[containing] the history of humankind as well as all manner of spiritual information.

Closer to our current era, a great deal of contemporary information on the Akashic Records has been made available...Perhaps the most extensive source of [recent] information regarding Akashic Records comes from the clairvoyant work of Edgar Cayce (1877-1945), Christian mystic and founder of A.R.E....When asked about the source of his information, Cayce replied that there were essentially two: The first was the subconscious mind of the individual for whom he was giving the [Life] reading and the second was the [person's] Akashic Records.

Kevin J. Todeschi
Edgar Cayce on the Akashic Records

Taking It Easy

Now that we understand Akashic Records, let's return to the prebirth chart. Position 20 means that relatively few predestined events will come our way. Choosing a low position means mostly relying on our own initiative and dealing with random events, but we forfeit certain protections when we aim so low. We will probably not be shielded from some freak occurrences, such as a brick dropped from a bridge and crashing through the windshield while driving 70 MPH on the freeway. As this example illustrates, being wide open to random events is not always a good thing.

Position 20 appeals to lazy people and hedonists, but enlightened entities—who just left a treacherous life—can also find 20 pretty darn attractive. Daniel may remind them that it is OK to pick 20, but it will probably mean a wasted life in terms of spiritual advancement. These souls need not fill out forms, because failure to sign means an automatic default to 20.

The Contracts of Evil Souls

Evil souls typically turn their backs on all this. As a result, they also default to position 20. Because they are allowed to exercise free will, they are permitted to entrench themselves further into darkness while accumulating an ever greater karmic debt, up to a certain point. Denial figures prominently for these souls: They prefer to believe that their wicked ways will advance their material lives and to Hell with the consequences.

Evil souls who pick 20 also predictably fail to factor in the law of cause and effect. They approach life with a recklessness that leads to amassing an even more ominous liability. So, for all the material success they may enjoy, they are never exempt from the workings of karma. By defaulting to 20, they still face the repercussions of their previous actions because they, too, carry forward their karmic standing from one life to the next.

However, if one's cumulative debt balloons to an unwieldy size, the rules change. Those possessing an overwhelming liability might expect to repeat conditions similar to their previous life, but are routinely assigned a 55+ life in a faraway land instead. They did not consent to such an extreme, but karmic obligations factor into the circumstances of some incarnations. Furthermore, colossal arrears may override a soul's choices when selecting their contract's terms, as we discussed earlier. These guidelines stay in force until the soul's karmic debt diminishes to a certain level. Only then is the soul's *afterlife* free will reinstated.

However, regardless of how massive or miniscule a soul's deficit, free will on Earth remains intact.

Nefarious souls thus involuntarily surrender their afterlife free will regarding the circumstances of their next life. Their immense karmic cargo overshadows all else and unconditional free will is re-established only after they have significantly paid down their balance due. This reminds me of the released felon who must fulfill many restrictions imposed by her parole before she can rejoin society on the same terms as before.

The difference between voluntarily choosing a high number and having a difficult life forced upon us relates to how we fare in adversity. The volunteer enters the situation on a much higher plane and eventually recognizes how spiritually saturated the experience is. Those drafted against their wills go through adversities as well, but usually miss the point. Even if most of the people around them "get it," this understanding rarely rubs off.

Evil thrives everywhere, yet malevolent souls may not account for a large part of any given population. Nevertheless, they are surely as entrenched in hardship as their more evolved counterparts. Faced with extreme torment, these spiritual slugs will be more likely to figure out a way to exploit the situation (and acquire even greater karmic arrears) than to be enveloped by the love around them and do some good for a change. If they fail to turn around, their next astral life and future incarnations will be even more miserable than the previous ones until they have significantly improved their karmic standing.

Selecting the Degree of Suffering

Let's return to Daniel and his chart. Most of us in Western countries have chosen a position between 30 and 50. In these cases, Daniel relies solely on crash-cart materials. With the first form, we acknowledge full understanding that whatever level we choose, we are consenting to the *degree of suffering* and not to the specifics. We are *not* consenting to:

- An abusive spouse

- Terminal cancer at 22 years of age
- The accidental drowning death of our six-year-old daughter
- Lengthy imprisonment for a crime we did not commit.

On this consent form we are leaving the specifics to a Higher Power and we trust that, whatever we face, we will be equipped to handle it. Taking responsibility for painful situations refers to this agreement. Yes, we did sign up for this much pain. True, we never would have asked for *this* situation. However, we did know that the position we chose might include such circumstances.

If we forgot all this during the transition from our previous life, it was certainly pounded back into our minds during the refresher courses. We could not have passed the tests without reciting all the possibilities for each position, such as 20, 30, 40, etc. This would have been followed up by a second test, examining our knowledge of our chosen position.

In conclusion, we simply never learn what form our adversities will take before we leave the afterlife. We only understand the range of possibilities assigned to each degree of pressure. Unfortunately, we are then forced to deal with the quadriplegia, the severe autism, the cheating spouse, the mudslide-damaged house, the relentless loneliness, the genetic predisposition to addiction, and so on.

If we then decide to take responsibility for our circumstances in life, we have gone a long way toward growing up spiritually. This admission can lead us to make the most of a bad situation and can bring us to the point of full resolution, or at least a marked improvement in some other area of our life. Whether our spiritual growth manifests itself in a worldly improvement is far from guaranteed. Remember the old Zen adage: "Before enlightenment, the laundry. After enlightenment, the laundry."

Before we resume this discussion, I would like to mention as a counterpoint, the Buddhist perspective on suffering. In a nutshell, Buddhists believe that virtually all of our misery is attributable to us. They never factor in God or Buddha as sources of adversity. Moreover, the acceptance of full responsibility for a given plight informs much of the Buddhist teachings. Within the North American culture, some of us recoil from this philosophy. However, if we search deep within, we may indeed acknowledge this as true most of the time.

Benevolent Forces and Invisible Protection

Let's now discuss common features of the positions on the scale between 20 and 80.

First, let's look at ethereal protection, which requires different types of safeguards relative to our position on the scale. The higher the number, the more vigilant are our angels. (I use the term "angel" to denote invisible, benevolent forces.) If we choose 70, perhaps we have several angels. They keep us going by constantly bolstering our survival instinct and by offering soothing comfort when necessary. We rarely perceive such assistance, but sometimes we can become dangerously exhausted, and so sick of a situation that we feel death might be welcome. At such times, we may inexplicably revive and find the strength to carry on. These are the angels at work in extreme situations.

At level 40, I imagine that one angel is assigned to each of us. These entities occasionally revive their charges and offer consolation as well, but they are most often on the lookout for adverse situations that do not fit the blueprint we chose. It is their job to figure out ways to avoid some random event that would take us off track.

These angels function in much the same way that a competent driver does. The motorist spots an obstacle a few miles ahead and adjusts his position accordingly. Angels also operate on a preemptive basis. In some instances, these angels even call for backup. A fictional story of a toddler's fall from a balcony demonstrates the work of a troop of angels.

The Toddler and the Mattress

A two-year-old fell from a fourth-story balcony 40 minutes after a man put a mattress on the sidewalk for trash pickup. The mattress meant the difference between life-threatening injuries and minor ones. A group of angels had quickly evaluated the situation an hour earlier. They scurried through the building looking for something to break the baby's fall. One whispered into the ear of the man with the mattress, "Put the mattress outside. Go on, do it now."

When the man returned home, his wife said, "I thought trash pickup was tomorrow afternoon." The man answered, "I know, but I felt I had to do it now."

The angels had averted the catastrophe without breaking any natural laws. Awestruck witnesses called it a "miracle." Indeed, the angels saved the baby, his parents, and possibly the landlord from a world of trouble. Such trauma *at this point, in this form*, would have been completely at odds with what those four souls had signed up for.

Overworked Angels

Let's switch from position 40 to 20. The angels on this level operate like workers in an overtaxed social services system. People in the 20-25 ranges have agreed to random events, but many of them still have some degree of commitment to their spiritual development. So, one overworked angel is assigned to many people in this relatively easy range. These angels operate on a *triage* basis, so who knows if this angel can be in the right place at the right time for any given person? It is part of the crapshoot that goes with choosing a number that has such a high incidence of randomness.

We have discussed our astral-plane contracts at length in this chapter. We have also demonstrated how pitiful the law-of-attraction's possibilities are in light of just one of the laws of transition. Along with our prebirth agenda, our sacred purpose is likewise determined before we incarnate. In the next chapter, we will examine how they work together.

What really matters most? The perfection of His mighty symphony or our own remarkably clever performance of that difficult passage for the tenth violin? If the composition requires our silence, are we more concerned with the snub administered or the mystery and beauty of God's orchestration?

Evelyn Underhill
The Spiritual Life

Chapter 6

The Laws of Transition—Our Sacred Purpose

Common wisdom dictates that everyone is assigned a purpose. I believe this is true, but when the time comes to carry it out some of us turn our backs on the opportunity because free will can always override the fulfillment of a purpose.

Parenting

For most of us, parenting serves as our main purpose, yet we still hear about mothers leaving their newborns on church steps and fathers running away during the pregnancy. Conversely, we see very young parents rise to the challenge and mature tremendously during the child's first year. Fortunately, responsible parents account for the vast majority. Raising children—so they can learn lessons and fulfill their own mandates—may be more spiritually valuable than other sacred designations.

Adults who feel damaged by dysfunctional parents were intentionally paired with these particular souls because of the terms of their prebirth contract. In these cases, the parents perform two functions. Along with child rearing, they serve as the child's first chance to learn lessons through the introduction of aggravating people in their life. Let's take a closer look.

Malicious Parents

Dysfunctional parents can be characterized as either benign or malicious. Cruelty inflicted on a child by a parent most often manifests as abuse or neglect. If this heartlessness results from an addiction, then these parents effectively put the whole thing in motion each time they take a drink or open a casino door. Of course, accountability and growing karmic debt go along with each instance of parental misconduct.

Some children are forced into the position of parenting the parent, so this adult has ostensibly robbed the child of the many pleasures associated with childhood and may have also impaired the child's potential at school.

We need not discuss this further because abuse and neglect are much easier to spot than the insidious symptoms associated with the benign, but misguided, parent. At first, we rarely perceive mistakes made by an otherwise caring parent.

Benign Parents

Like my mother, most seemingly innocuous parents are actually motivated by love and could never imagine harming their child in any way. My mother took care of me properly and fulfilled all of the obvious parental commitments. She bore no traces of either an intellect or a sense of humor, so right there we had our first conflicts. However, had these been the only issues, I am sure I would have been OK.

Influenced by her deeply ingrained Victorian sensibility, my mother ruled through silence. As we have already discussed, her directives came in the form of raised eyebrows and scornful expressions, which conveyed derision and disapproval in a way that cut to the core.

In chapter 4, we investigated how this kind of parenting inadvertently erects gigantic obstructions in adulthood, which in turn thwart our ability to attain our goals. These blockages may even prevent us from serving our purpose because they sometimes stunt the spiritual growth necessary to make us strong enough for the task.

As dysfunctional parents, any steps we take to increase awareness about these issues could result in spiritual advances for us, and an enriched life for our children. One way to approach this would entail listening to and observing our children because we may unearth some valuable clues.

As children of messed-up parents, we cannot expect miracles. However, we can recognize that most parents unwittingly repeat cycles from their own childhoods and that most of our complaints refer to *their* unconscious issues. Forgiveness—along with a persistent resolve to break this cycle—forms the foundation for great spiritual advances in this area.

The Enlightened Soul

Some of us serve a Divine purpose by just being ourselves. Imagine a highly evolved individual, whom I will name Melanie for the sake of this discussion. She lives among people who are in great need of spiritual advice. Melanie shares a lifestyle similar to the people around her and works at a comparable job.*

Melanie's wisdom allows her to introduce people to new ways of looking at life. Although her ideas might astound some of her neighbors from time to time, Melanie has unwittingly become their primary spiritual teacher.† For example, she may offer a truly inspired take on the value of forgiveness. This may or may not influence someone who needs to forgive, but at least they have found an alternative way of looking at their situation.

Not everyone welcomes spiritual advice, so Melanie's worldview is lost on some people. Others, however, benefit enormously from Melanie's presence in their community. Her assistance can lead to good outcomes at best, and an increase in knowledge at worst. Melanie instructs by her own example, which is always more powerful than words. Some may choose to disregard her, but others allow her guidance to sink in and change the course of their lives as a result. Based on a true story, the HBO movie

---

* The enlightened soul often takes the form of a wise elder.

† I say "unwittingly" because we rarely can distinguish between events that refer to our purpose and those that relate to other issues.

Lackawanna Blues (2005) portrays just such a person and the dozens of people whose lives were made better because of her. [37]

Melanie exemplifies someone whose most significant purpose spans her entire adult life. However, our spiritual blueprint can also be manifested in incidents of much shorter duration sprinkled throughout our lives. We can be in the right place at the right time with offers of an organ transplant, much needed consolation, or even something as simple as jumper cables.

The Impact of Small Acts of Kindness

Jumper cables may not seem significant at first, but we never know what kind of an impact a small act might have.

For example, I get heatstroke at the drop of a hat and I was trying to get home one day while it was 92 degrees with high humidity. My car would not start, but I got help within five minutes. A kind man with jumper cables essentially pre-empted a nasty bout of heatstroke, but he had no way of knowing that. His simple act of kindness was more important to me than he could possibly have guessed. Such small acts can get someone out of a bad situation fast enough to avoid serious problems, or to arrive somewhere in time for a beneficial experience that would not have been possible with a delay.

These are tiny examples, but they add up and carry weight in the scheme of things. Moreover, small stuff comprises more of the fabric of our lives than the big, defining moments. Needless to say, rising to these occasions bolsters our karmic standing, regardless of their apparent insignificance at the time.

The Angel of Highway 219

In a similar vein, let me recount a strange story that took place early in my spiritual development. When I lived in New York State, Highway 219 connected Buffalo to my home 50 miles to the south. At that time, I drove an old rust bucket that frequently got stuck in snow. I was amazed at how quickly people with tire chains would stop to help me. Not one of them would ever accept the paltry $10 I offered them for their trouble. By the time I could afford to fix my car I had been bailed out a dozen times and a new winter had begun.

With more reliable transportation, I decided to return all the favors. I was determined to stop for any car in distress to offer either a ride or a jumpstart. One night I saw an SUV stopped on the side of the road. I pulled up behind it, but when I took a few steps towards the vehicle, it took off. I mentioned this incident to my friend Lisa and added that I was not going to allow this failed payback attempt to discourage me. "I want to be the Angel of the 219," I told her. "Whatever it takes, I'm going to help people."

When this exact situation was repeated two more times I became quite mystified. By then, I only had to open my car door and the SUV would take off. I wanted to take down the license plate number so that I would not bother with this vehicle again. After all, the SUV was in good enough shape to leave quickly, so it did not need assistance. Because it was always dark when these incidents occurred, I not only could not see the license plate, I also could not even identify the model or color. The next time I saw Lisa, I sputtered, "I'm going to help people, damn it!"

Throughout that winter, the Angel of the 219 stopped 14 times and the SUV took off each and every time. I eventually concluded that it had to be the same vehicle over and over, but I could never fathom what was going on.

The mystery was solved a year later after I had moved out of the area. A friend of Lisa's told her about Ginny, her coworker. Ginny had been married for 11 years when she began an affair with Ryan, a married work associate. They had been carpooling in Ryan's Explorer and one thing had led to another. Yes, the people in the SUV had been Ryan and Ginny going at it after work.

Ginny complained to her friend about a "cop" who often pulled up behind them. Ryan would argue that it could not be the police because he never saw lights or heard sirens, but Ryan could never be sure because the bright lights from the "cop's" car made it impossible to be certain.

"Well, who else could that be?" Ginny would insist. "It might be an unmarked vehicle."

As Ginny recounted the tale, she complained that every other time they were making out, this damn cop would pull up and all the fun would be over.

"And this went on for months!" Ginny complained.

Ginny also explained that Ryan always parked about a quarter of a mile past a particular exit, which is exactly where the Angel of the 219 found the SUV every time.

In the end, neither Ginny nor Ryan felt comfortable with motels, so when their relationship soured a bit on other fronts, they broke up.

After 14 failed attempts to help, the Angel of the 219 hung up her wings for good when she moved out of state.

The Purpose of Talent

As we saw with the Angel of the 219, I felt a strong obligation to repay those who had assisted me in the past, so I assigned myself a purpose— to no avail.

Similarly, creative people sometimes desperately want their main purpose to be tied into their talent, but they have no more control over realizing their purpose than did the Angel of the 219. We cannot *force* a purpose to materialize. When the time comes, the appropriate circumstances will manifest for us. Only then can we exercise free will to either reject or to take advantage of a given opportunity.

The most common question asked by people with unacknowledged talent is, "Why would God give me this talent unless He wanted me to use it?" The person who asks this reveals three things about herself:

First, she is blind to the bigger picture: Her life will probably span many decades, yet she may be addressing this in her 20s or 30s.

Second, she refuses to acknowledge that she can express her talent immediately if she wants to. Nothing substantial prevents her from writing, painting, dancing, or joining a regional acting group right now. Her talent does not have to be acknowledged by others before she can use it.

Third, impatience and frustration cloud her perception about the realities of her chosen career path, such as:

- Even when artists show tremendous promise, their early works are often raw and unrefined compared to later ones, which are far richer in form, substance, and nuance
- Creative fields are so crowded with talented individuals that most successful artists have waited a very long time to make a living from their creativity alone.

Many cases of delayed recognition end up yielding rewards beyond our wildest expectations and often materialize when we are better prepared to handle all the madness of fame. If we have spent a very long time refining our craft, we will have developed such a stable and deeply rooted talent that retaining our professional standing should be a lot easier.

Creativity and Our Dreams of Fulfillment

Accomplishing our creative goals turns out to be similar to realizing any other wish—most gifted people must do a lot of spiritual work before things fall into place. The more we grow spiritually, the less likely we will succumb to the infantile behavior and/or destructive tendencies we sometimes associate with success. Furthermore, early success conceals a nasty side effect, as author Albert Goldman explains:

> No man is really changed by success. Success works on a man's personality like a truth drug, bringing him out of the closet and revealing...what was always inside his head.
>
> Albert Goldman
> Montana and Smith
> *Overnight*

Goldman's theory illustrates that we run the risk of becoming frozen in place if great success comes to us when we are spiritually ill equipped to handle it well. Psychologist Belisa Vranich would add that celebrity status makes us vulnerable to "acquired narcissism," a term she has coined to describe an ever increasing sense of self-absorption, the longer one sustains fame.[38]

For example, celebrities find themselves surrounded by yes-men and others who constantly reinforce the same message: "You are a very special person with a unique and unmatched talent." Special privileges and relentless deferential treatment accumulate over time and ultimately produce egomania in an otherwise reasonably well-adjusted person. Dr. Drew Pinsky qualifies Vranich's theory by adding, "More commonly, a person's pre-existing narcissistic tendencies eventually bloom into full-blown narcissism through sustained celebrity status." (paraphrased)[39]

We sometimes see actors with longstanding careers who do not fit into this theory because their spiritually precocious nature pre-empted the otherwise immature characteristics. For these precious few—relative to countless celebrities who fit the self-important profile—their creativity does not conflict with their spiritual agenda. In other words, their forum for predetermined lessons often falls outside this framework.

Furthermore, we frequently see a purpose unfold in some cases that could not have been fulfilled without the attendant fame. Such is the case with some celebrities involved in charity fundraising. (I say "some" because certain celebrities see fundraising as merely a self-promotion opportunity, while others express a sincere interest in endorsing a given charity.)

The Life Review

When successful creative people evaluate their lives afterwards, they are subject to the same criteria as we are, but within an altered context. These life reviews emphasize their *responses* to a situation, not the situation itself. Hence, successful artists' end-of-life assessments could contain the following questions:

- How far into self-indulgence did I sink when particular contracts endorsed diva-like perks, or when my net worth reflected unprecedented wealth?
- Did I preserve as much honor and integrity in my new life as I had before success struck?
- Did I treat the people around me more like partners, or like minions doing my bidding?
- Did I allow myself to exploit sycophants, who were willing to pander to even the most unspeakable hedonistic activities?
- Did my behaviors conform to the priorities and values I once used as a guide to get through life?
- If applicable, did I maintain fidelity when so many temptations emerged?

We can derive several conclusions from this line of questioning:

First, success and wealth present so many opportunities to waver from our spiritual foundations that we can harvest a new meaning from: "Be careful what you wish for."

Second, accomplished artists often fail these challenges and their deviations unfavorably influence their karmic standing.

Third, recognition of talent rarely fulfills a higher purpose by itself. Rather, rewarded talent most often paves the way to accomplishing heavenly works through direct action, if we are evolved enough to recognize this.

Waiting Forever versus Everything Falling into Place

Let's return to the people who have yet to meaningfully express their gift. We will know when our sacred purpose is tied into our talent because everything will fall into place to make things happen. For example, some concert pianists were raised in musical families and had no problem getting full scholarships to prestigious music programs, which led to the beginnings of major careers.

The next example involves the work itself as Divine execution. Sometimes a particular work may serve a Divine purpose but may require a successful artist to execute it. As a child, Steven Spielberg made quite a few short films. He was able to prepare for his huge career early in life because his parents supported his adolescent filmmaking experiments. Spielberg's fame evidently allowed for *Schindler's List* in a way that would not have been possible without his celebrity. *Schindler's List* probably fulfilled Spielberg's main purpose as it relates to his talent.[40]

Schindler's List may never have been possible without Spielberg's fame behind it because it contains several noncommercial elements. Shot mostly in black and white, *Schindler's List* features many disturbing sequences. Furthermore, the film informs us that Schindler's life after the war was very difficult, which disappoints an audience's expectations of rewards for a man who saved approximately 1,200 people from Nazi annihilation.

Each of these examples illustrates how situations—particularly in childhood—are conducive to making our creative purpose in life possible. At the same time, less obvious opportunities to fulfill spiritual mandates may also be sprinkled throughout these people's lives.

Sadly for most of us, our gifts may not have been nurtured at home and circumstances did not pave an easy path towards dream fulfillment. For us, an uphill battle ensues when we persist in pursuing our goals. This means that our sacred agreement calls for impressive spiritual growth *before* we achieve significant recognition. As long as our desires clash with our current reality, we experience the anguish of extreme frustration. As we know by now, chronic pain of any kind allows us to flourish spiritually. Therefore, unacknowledged talent is as worthy a spiritual platform as any other.

Let's now look at unusual examples of purposes with a twist.

Purpose with a Twist—The Gastric Bypass

When I was in my early 20s, I was admitted to the hospital for a gastric bypass. The procedure was brand new at that time and a prudent doctor would never have recommended it for most patients because the risks outweighed the benefits to a frightening degree. I had proposed the bypass to a surgeon who was quite reluctant and he tried to dissuade me. When he realized how serious I was, he sent me to the hospital for an entire week of pre-surgical testing.

My hospital roommate, Doris, had had most of her intestines removed due to cancer a few years earlier and suffered from ongoing post-op complications. This 60-year-old woman spent her days perusing stacks of magazines, looking for pictures of food. Doris could no longer eat real food and her diet offered a single menu item five times a day: A nutrition drink compounded by a pharmacist. Yum. At least 10 times a day, Doris would show me a picture of an entrée while she recalled the taste and texture or recounted some experience she had enjoyed while eating that item. I was reminded of a blind person remembering images from the days when she could see.

As the week wore on, my medical tests became more invasive and increasingly unpleasant. Then came the time to sign the surgery consent forms. I simply could not do it. I told the nurse and the doctor that maybe it was too big a risk and used Doris as the main reason for my decision. I soon interpreted the looks on their faces as very knowing, as if my refusal to sign had been their goal all along. Evidently, they had paired me with Doris as a deterrent.

This situation did not carry the same meaning as the toddler-and-the-balcony tale, because the hospital story was all about warnings in relation to free will. My angels understood that their task here called for caution, not circumvention.

We can deduce the following from this experience:

- Doris had no idea that she was serving a purpose
- My angels may have rigged it so that I was shielded from a more shortsighted doctor
- I may have faced far more serious post-op complications than would have been the case today, but it is still a pretty daunting

procedure and I remain intimidated by it

- Catastrophic complications probably would have knocked me off track for good.

Another story illustrates the inexplicable mysteries associated with fulfilling purposes.

Purpose with a Twist—The Researcher

At the age of 59, Pere Jamme had amassed mountains of material charting the language and history of Yemen as it was in 1500 BC. This Belgian-born priest was one of four scholars, each of whom worked on different facets of the same project. None of them had the benefit of computers in 1975, so their findings were all on paper. Without warning, 35 years of Jamme's research was destroyed by fire. However, his reaction to the devastation was far more intriguing than the event itself.

"I know there is a great lesson in this," Jamme said, "but I don't know what it is."

Daunted but determined, Jamme forged on.

"The Lord doesn't ask me for success," Jamme said. "He only asks me to work. Work He is going to get. The rest is His business."[41]

Author Evelyn Underhill might add that we sometimes feel like tools, picked up when needed and used in unexpected ways. By the time we realize we have not been consulted, we have been put back in the toolbox. Sometimes we are cogs in a giant wheel, or "lowly subordinates" doing the "same monotonous job, year in and year out." So, we must take our small place "in God's vast operation, instead of trying to run a poky little business on our own."[42]

Before we finish discussing our sacred purpose, I want to add a few concluding thoughts:

First, if we realize a big dream only after an agonizingly long time, rest assured that we have grown spiritually in the interim.

Second, we can be living out our Divine script and not even realize it, as would be the case for parents whose sole purpose is raising children.

Third, we have no control over selecting the specifics of our purpose. However, we are always asked if we will accept one and a chosen few are asked if they are willing to serve at their maximum level of stress. For example, if we choose the difficult position 70 on the spiritual growth chart, then our purpose will be served under the most extreme circumstances allowable for level 70.

The late Christopher Reeve's (1952-2004) life following his horseback-riding accident probably falls into this category, yet his life before the accident was far milder by comparison, according to *Still Me*, his autobiography.

Reeve's work after his accident brought spinal cord injuries out of obscurity and into mainstream consciousness. This may never have happened without him. In interviews given during the last years of their lives, Reeve and his wife, the late Dana Reeve (1961-2006), gave the impression that they had a clear understanding of their purpose. (Had they lived long enough, we can only imagine what they would have said about *The Secret.*)

Symptoms for Figuring out the Source of Distress

Even with heightened awareness, it can be next to impossible to determine whether a given situation refers to karma, purpose, a mirroring of our own characteristics, or prebirth agenda issues.

For example, after substantially upgrading my living situation, I was still faced with a landlady who had a very cavalier attitude, as mentioned earlier. Whenever an issue needed resolution and she did not like the choices, she offered to terminate the lease with no regard for my situation or the feasibility of her other options. Her utter insensitivity towards me made me nuts. Her basic theme was: "You are only useful to me as long as you are so low maintenance that you are nearly invisible."

This situation bewildered me because, by then, my consciousness had expanded enough that my own imperious attitude had been superseded by sensitivity to others. Consequently, I knew she was not mirroring me or my situation. Since my problems with her did not serve any purpose, I was left with prebirth agenda and karma as the possible causes. After considerable deliberation, it occurred to me that I had hurt many people over the years with a trivializing attitude, so it seemed appropriate that I had a karmic debt in that area. Therefore, every time my landlady dismissed me, I may have been paying back at the rate of one offense at a time.

This particular insight represents one of a precious few in my life. In most cases, I have been unable to interpret events as they were unfolding, in terms of purpose, agenda, etc. This tells me that *responding* to a situation is far more important than identifying its source.

As we go through an ordeal, we may understand that this *must* refer to a lesson, but we usually cannot specify which one. Upon reflection years later, much can be learned in hindsight. The passage of time helps us see exactly which lessons these situations and people represented.

I have included an exercise in the Appendix for identifying the spiritual roles of the people and situations in our lives. This quiz can shed light on issues that are ripe for change and can be used as a tool for evaluating troubling elements in a fresh and unusual way.

Chapter 7

The Law of Cause and Effect—Karma

We have so far discussed suffering and the law of attraction in terms of our prebirth agenda and our sacred purpose, as well as several unconscious factors, but the plot thickens when the intricacies of karma are thrown into the mix.

Theories about karma vary from one religion to another and among numerous cultures. Many cultures embrace karma as the impersonal underpinning of *all* interrelationships, including those among flora, fauna, and other natural phenomena. Indeed, some cultures ramp it up to include absolutely all actions/reactions within the universe. In any case, even the simplest interpretation implies mysterious and complex forces at work.[43]

Regardless of the cultural variations, when we focus on the karma associated with spiritual growth virtually all versions talk about karma in terms of cause and effect instead of reward and punishment. This chapter focuses on the westernized version of karmic theory, which is concerned almost exclusively with personal development.[44]

Generally speaking, our spiritual crimes and misdemeanors in one life are usually addressed in that life, but a carryover to the next life could also occur. However, when we experience anguish it is impossible to tell if this refers to karma or to the other elements we discussed earlier.

Karmically Induced Regressions

We are rarely able to distinguish between karmic influences and the other factors that can affect our experiences. Our ignorance is the single biggest factor we must consider when we talk about trusting the Universe or maintaining our faith during hard times. When we close one door, the next one to open may not lead us to desirable situations. In fact, we occasionally find ourselves moving backwards or sinking into a noxious abyss.

We cannot control the inner workings of karma or the other factors and we cannot always prevent the onset of a nasty situation. However, we can influence, and favorably alter, our karmic standing by performing redemptive acts based on our mindfulness of the world around us. Redemptive acts are strictly voluntary and therefore refer to those rare occasions when free will reigns and we are partially in control of this vast and intricate system.

Redemption and Karma

I am reminded of the 2002 CBS series *Hack,* which starred David Morse as Mike Olshansky, a disgraced police officer. When Mike was caught stealing $8,000, he refused to implicate his partner and took all the heat himself. He lost his job, his home, and his wife. His son's subsequent uncertainty and ambivalence towards him replaced years of unwavering love and admiration.

Mike drove a taxi, and he constantly helped his passengers and other people he met. I saw these episodes as terrific examples of redemption in action because Mike went to great lengths to assist others, often taking scary risks. The best part was that Mike seemed so driven by his desire to win back his son that he did not perceive the link between his actions and their influence on the bigger picture. This meant that the love for his son was his only motivation.

Overall, the scenarios in *Hack* seem completely feasible in theory, but the consistent amount of drama involved rings truer in fiction than in real life. Nevertheless, we can bolster our understanding of redemption in relation to karma through Mike Olshansky's character. Let's examine Mike's story using the three hallmarks of karma: Motive, sacrifice, and impact on others.

Motive

If Mike had a self-serving motive, it was not clear to the viewer. He seemed so shaken by the fallout from his spiraling descent that he felt compelled to make up for his mistakes just because it was the right thing to do, as if his moral compass had only been dislodged temporarily.

Sacrifice

The degree of sacrifice varied from one situation to another, but the potential costs only made Mike pause and re-evaluate things briefly before he acted. In the end, he always agreed to help. Of course, this had something to do with the freedom fiction enjoys over real life. In reality, it is OK to let self-preservation kick in at times, even if it aborts an opportunity for a redemptive act.

Impact

The assistance Mike gave to others had a tremendous impact on their lives. Even when we make allowances for the difference between fiction and reality, the show's depiction of karmic repercussions was very impressive. The series led the viewer to believe that Mike never lost an opportunity to help others, regardless of the risk involved.

In one episode, Mike moved Heaven and Earth to recover thousands of dollars lost by one of his passengers. Mike was misled into believing the money was intended for a worthy cause. At the end of the episode, Mike watched the passenger disappear into an apartment building with the recovered cash. We then saw what Mike did not: The passenger used the money to gamble in a card game.

In this example, Mike's intention salvaged the situation. Mike thought the positive results would be much greater than they actually were, so if he had been a real person working off a karmic debt he would have received full credit for his effort despite the less desirable outcome.

When we help people for no other reason than that the opportunity presents itself, we gain karmic reward points. We also demonstrate an understanding that all people are connected to us in some way, as our actions imply some kind of tie to the person we help. This link applies to even the smallest acts of kindness.

Redemptive acts also offer us a glimpse into the mystifying inner workings of karma, which rarely play out on a tit-for-tat basis. Mike's embezzlement was never mirrored by the circumstances in which he found himself, yet his handling of the situations most definitely qualified for karmic credit. Similarly, when all else fails, we can always rely on selfless acts of kindness as foolproof ways of diminishing our karmic debt.

Karma as Currency

Karmic transactions are similar to exchanges of money. For example, money is the neutral entity between a paycheck and a purchase. We earn a paycheck, convert it into cash, and use the money to buy things. Our impersonal karmic bank account operates in much the same way. It applies to all of us equally, regardless of how miniscule or massive our karmic debts may be, just as supermarket prices do not fluctuate relative to the customer: Both sexual predators and rabbinical students pay exactly the same amount for a loaf of bread.

Clearly, only a few exceptional souls turn up in every century with a substantial credit balance at the end of their lives. Most of these people do such extraordinary things that they become historical figures, such as Saint Teresa and Gandhi. Though their karmic standing at birth may have been a liability, it changed into a credit balance later on.

What Goes Around Comes Around

People often think of the saying "what goes around comes around" as equivalent to karma, but how many times have we actually seen, for example, a swindler being defrauded later in life? An exact match for karmic payback is quite rare. However, close matches do occur. I remember somebody writing about a serial arsonist returning as a nurse on a burn ward.

A Skeleton in the Basement

Allow me to digress with a real-life example of the literal view of karma, which I saw in a true-crime story.

A man moved into a house in Venice Beach, California. During renovations, the new homeowner discovered human remains buried in the basement and called the police. The skull had been so extremely bludgeoned that it was in several pieces.

The forensic anthropologists had never seen anything so brutal and concluded that the victim's pain would have been beyond imagining. They were able to establish the age of the remains, the approximate age of the victim, etc., and this helped police to identify the remains as female and to pinpoint the actual homeowner at the time of the murder. We will call him Bryan.

Before long, the police located witnesses who remembered a woman who had once lived at Bryan's, The woman had disappeared, never to be seen again. Bryan soon became the only suspect and the police successfully tracked him down.

When the detectives discovered Bryan was a resident at a convalescent home, they were not surprised. Given the date of the crime, they had expected him to be at least 70 years old. However, they were taken aback when they finally met him. Bryan had been rendered a blithering idiot by a freak accident. Many years earlier, something heavy had fallen from a high-rise building and smacked him on the head, creating severe and irreversible brain damage.

I was struck by this story because it featured the rare occurrence of eye-for-an-eye karmic retribution. Ordinarily, we really must make a distinction between karma as a whole and the idea that "what goes around comes around," because it simply does not "come around" in such a literal fashion very often.

Vengeance Is Mine

The following Biblical passage has resonated deeply within me for a long time now: "'Vengeance is mine,' said The Lord."

If we take this seriously, we are trusting that those who have done us harm will get theirs in the end because God or the Universe will take care of it for us. Of course, regardless of how we phrase it, we are really talking about karma. However, we are rarely around to enjoy such reckonings.

Taking this Bible passage to heart and *not* acting in a vengeful way preserves our karmic standing. If we resist the temptation to act, we avoid the karmic fallout from whatever we were planning to do. Yes, even when we seem to be justified, we incur bad karma by launching vengeful acts. I do not really know if justification converts into a mitigating factor, but I am sure we still have some sort of Hell to pay for the revenge we transform from thought into action. I also know that we can all live better if we stop accruing more karmic debt.

Here is another aspect of vengeance to consider: If we confine revenge to the realm of dreams and imaginings, we may be safe on the karma front but we are slowly poisoning our spiritual essence. Our soul and spirit together occupy a fixed amount of spiritual real estate on this plane of existence. The more we fill it up with negativity, the less room we have for positive things, including constructive experiences and opportunities that might come our way. We are not completely blocking out the potential good, but rather significantly limiting it. In addition, some things—such as cherished relationships—simply perish in a hostile environment.

Over time, bitterness and vengeful thinking produce an alarming number of contaminants that eventually leak out to infect other areas of our lives. Though the process is always reversible, the damage might not be. Therefore, nurturing hostility never harms the target of our vengeance, but always does damage within us. The longer we hold onto these poisons, the more we put ourselves at risk for life-threatening illnesses in addition to the spiritual and emotional problems already discussed. In the end, it is our spiritual duty to purge this type of thinking as soon as we possibly can.

Karma and *The Secret*

The last discussion is about as close as this book gets to casting a favorable light on *The Secret's* emphasis on positive thinking all the time, no matter what.

Positive thinking is overrated because its influence is quite limited. As the previous discussion illustrates, replacing venomous thoughts with more constructive ones can only be a good thing. However, believing that we are only days away from happiness and satisfaction is tantamount to living in a fool's paradise (a place I have visited often, courtesy of the law of attraction) and may keep us from taking concrete steps to correct a dismal situation. Moreover, as we discussed in an earlier chapter, pessimists can get job promotions and negative thinkers can beat cancer.

Revenge—The Boomerang Effect

One of my earliest experiences with revenge contaminated me, but it also permanently cured me of vengeful thinking.

Someone once betrayed me in a way that was insulting and demeaning. I felt compelled to spew out my rage in a way that would, in turn, wound and diminish the other person. I succeeded because my tirade was extremely effective, but it immediately ricocheted. The toxins I sent out came straight back to drench my own soul. Spiritually speaking, I was sitting in my own filth for days afterward.

This outcome was so unexpected that it caught me completely off guard. Though I was only in my early 20s and 15 years away from my spiritual awakening, I learned this lesson well. Years later, I still find other people astonished by what they call my "self control." It is really self-preservation and my unwavering faith that the Universe will take care of things on my behalf.

Karma in Relation to Our Consciousness at a Given Time

Responsibility goes hand in hand with an expanding consciousness. Let's look at everyday examples to see how this works:

A three-year-old might see a disfigured person and loudly ask her father, "What's wrong with his face?" By the time she is 10, she will understand that this is not suitable behavior and will at least wait until the other person is out of earshot before saying anything. The 10-year-old knows a lot more than the toddler about such things. Therefore, the pre-adolescent must act according to the knowledge she has now, not as she would have acted years earlier. Throughout our lives, transgressions trigger karmic debts of varying sizes, depending on our consciousness at the time.

Getting back to my experience with exacting revenge: My temporary poisoning, followed by an all too slow detoxification, was all I needed to put my faith completely in the unknowable workings of the Universe when I felt compelled to lash out. Perhaps that instant contamination resulted in a thorough erasure of the karmic debt I undoubtedly incurred. Had I done such a nasty thing again after realizing the spiritual consequences of revenge, I imagine my debt would have been greater. If our actions fall short of our current level of awareness, we are sure to suffer more.

One final note about vengeance: Our irrational side can sometimes override our current state of awareness, causing us to commit a huge spiritual blunder. When we come to our senses, we are sometimes awash in remorse. If heartfelt, this regret tacitly acknowledges how serious the slip-up was and this realzation carries some weight in reducing our karmic liability for this particular action. Nonetheless, it does not exempt us from the residual effects, either in real life or in karmic terms.

For example, consider a vigilante who is otherwise a law-abiding citizen and a decent person. Overcome by anguish and irrationality, he takes the law into his own hands to exact revenge on an alleged perpetrator. No matter how much sincere remorse follows his vengeful act, he still must deal with both the legal and karmic repercussions. Accountability applies, even if the target of his revenge actually committed the crime in question.

Karma, Reincarnation, and Conflicting Beliefs

People who reject karma and reincarnation in favor of other beliefs are still subject to karmic laws and will experience multiple lives. In terms of spirituality, what we believe changes nothing as far as our prospective development is concerned.

For instance, suppose that some people do not believe that air exists. We cannot see air and the only evidence of its existence is wind. Scientists can prove that air exists, but breezes are only inferential side effects. Thus, for everyone else, it really is hard to verify. Still, we all depend on air for survival on this planet, whether we believe in it or not. And so it goes with the impersonal nature of both karma and reincarnation.

Even atheists are subject to these laws, though they would recoil from the very idea. When we think about it, atheists also run the gamut from primitive to evolved and from good to evil. Their beliefs set them apart, but I doubt that they incur any kind of penalty for rejecting God, because karma refers to conduct, not to beliefs.

Some people who believe in a Supreme Entity get angry with God for a very long time. Maybe something really bad happened to make them turn their backs on God. This, too, will not result in a karmic penalty because it arises from a certain level of consciousness and a misunderstanding of God's role. These people typically believe that God could have intervened, so they are angry that He did not. They have yet to understand that their level of suffering is something they signed up for and that their sorrow will lead them to unprecedented spiritual heights once they let go of the anger. They do not have to release the rage to please God, but rather to free themselves of the invisible ties that bind.

God almost certainly dismisses these rejections as signs of spiritual immaturity and is probably disappointed that angry souls do not take more responsibility for their own fate. After all, our most basic spiritual mandates include self-reliance and making the most of a bad situation, which includes dealing constructively with adversity and letting go of wrath. Over time, rage can be every bit as septic as a lengthy obsession with vengeance.

Karma and Suicide

As practiced in this society, many of our religions rank suicide a close second to murder as a major spiritual felony. However, when we factor in karma, the picture changes quite a bit. Let's consider this in light of the three facets of karma: Motive, impact on others, and degree of sacrifice.

Suicide: Motives

A suicidal person is almost always motivated by either physical or psychological agony and sees suicide as a way to end the anguish. Unfortunately, the pain this person is trying to escape does not go away. It is suspended intact until the next incarnation.

Whether we act upon them or not, suicidal thoughts imply:

- A lack of understanding about our well-informed consent to this particular life, troubles and all, before incarnation
- A refusal to acknowledge a precious opportunity to work through sorrow and achieve significant spiritual development

- An underdeveloped spirit who does not evaluate her hurt in relation to others who endure worse fates. Furthermore, the searing pain this soul is experiencing might be alleviated faster if she asked for spiritual or practical guidance. Professional help, or assistance from friends, would yield quicker results than prayer in many cases
- An inability to recognize that we always have a choice. It is true that a person in dire circumstances is probably choosing between bad and worse, but she does have options and is not locked into suicide as the only alternative.

Suicide and Legal Troubles

In the past 20 years of media coverage, I have heard of at least a dozen instances of suicides related to white-collar crimes. A person (usually a man) faces a sentence of 10+ years and the loss of his valued lifestyle. He cannot deal with the shame and ostracization, both of which he brought upon himself.

Suicide will degrade his karmic standing many times over. Had he sucked up the penalties and spent time in prison, his incarceration may have replenished his karmic bank account to one extent or another. Instead, he retains the liability associated with the crime and adds to it by suicide and its impact on everyone who loved him. To say that this kind of suicide represents a karmic can of worms would be a gross understatement.

Suicide: Impact on Others

Karmically speaking, the damage we do to our loved ones is truly the killer here. In upcoming incarnations, we will relive the grief our suicide has imposed on others. On the one hand, if the suicide only touched a few lives, this will limit the extent of our sorrow later on. On the other hand, if many people were immobilized by grief, our debt will be massive. Worse still, if just one person's life was ruined by the size and scope of their grief and the way it changed them...watch out.

Surviving a Parent's Suicide

Think of a child's reaction to a parent's suicide. A child's fragility is nothing to mess with and we cannot accurately forecast the outcome for a given child because we never know what someone will do in extreme circumstances.

Despite their reputation for resiliency, children have fewer coping mechanisms than adults, so the chances of devastation from a parent's suicide are quite high. We see this clearly when adults recall losing a parent in their formative years due to illness or accident. Though most of them adapted to life without that parent, their vivid scars attest to a continuous pain that they believe will never leave them. I cannot imagine how many times we multiply this for suicide.

Ordinary Things Can Mean a Lot

A man named Cooper recounted a simple but profound dream he had when he was depressed and considering suicide. Cooper dreamt he was at a picnic table in a park on a beautiful sunny day. He was with his 11-year-old son and the dream shifted to the boy's point of view. The son watched as Cooper ate, made small talk, and cleaned up the table. The pair then sat quietly for a while before Cooper woke up.

In an instant, Cooper understood the dream's meaning: His son needed him in his life and even the most mundane event meant something to the boy. At such a low point in Cooper's life, this dream influenced his perspective. Cooper felt he had to factor in the needs of both his son and daughter in any future thoughts of suicide. Cooper understood immediately that this dream was a wakeup call.

In retrospect, many years later, Cooper credits this dream as the single, biggest factor in turning his life around. It took Cooper a long time to dig out from under the mess his life had become, but this dream and Cooper's love for his children fueled his powers of endurance. Now that his life is substantially better, Cooper is very grateful to have understood the dream because he sees that he was only a few months (if not weeks) away from suicide at that time.

Suicide: The Degree of Sacrifice

Some argue that suicide is the coward's way out and that living is for the courageous, while others see it the opposite way. One thing I am sure of: Suicide is inherently selfish because it does not factor in the impact it will have on others. A suicidal person only knows that the pain must end at all costs. Therefore, sacrifice does not apply here.

Once in awhile we hear of a disguised suicide that was intended to help financially ravaged family members by enriching them through the decedent's bequest of life insurance proceeds. The person's objective may mitigate things only slightly, because the huge karmic consequences of self-annihilation virtually overshadow the suicide's good intentions. I am reminded of our earlier discussion of suicide as a way to avoid incarceration. In both instances, the once manageable karmic debts would be enlarged by suicide to a cumbersome size.

Suicide, Terminal Illnesses, and Assisted Suicide

Suicides prompted by end-of–life illnesses represent an entirely different story. Horrible diseases that produce unspeakable pain—along with a drastic reduction in quality-of-life factors—lead many people to consider suicide. Oftentimes, suicide had never been considered before the illness struck.

I believe that the spiritual caliber of a person's life to date would be the single biggest factor in determining the karmic outcome of such a suicide. Someone assisting suicide under these circumstances would theoretically incur greater karmic consequences than the patient. However, the assistant's life up to this point—in conjunction with his *innermost motives*—would go a long way to either expand or contract the debt.

The terminally ill person who commits suicide must still deal with the impact this will have on others, as with any other suicide. However, it is unlikely that many friends and relatives would respond to this type of suicide more negatively than to death by natural causes. In fact, some might even be relieved and grateful that the deceased's suffering was cut short.

In *Suicide: What Really Happens in the Afterlife?* John Klimo and Pamela Heath suggest that any self-inflicted death will result in a kind of death-sleep. The suicide will only awaken when the time between the moment of his suicide and his projected natural death has finally passed. Hence, a terminally ill suicide's "sleep" is far shorter than that of a healthy suicide.[45]

Murder/Suicide

A murder/suicide invites an even more serious karmic debt than would one murder followed by a suicide years later. In this case, the whole is vastly greater than the sum of its parts. The perpetrator must relive not only the murder and the grief of all the survivors combined, but must also incur a separate and substantial debt for involving another person in a purely egocentric and destructive act. The question will be: "If you wanted to commit suicide, why did you have to take someone else with you?" In the end, murder/suicide represents the height of selfishness within this discussion.

The Suicidally Inclined

Before we leave this section, I would like to directly address suicidally inclined readers. If you were to research in depth the spiritual and afterlife consequences of suicide, you would understand that I have barely scratched the surface here.

You would also have the bejeezus kicked out of you because mountains of evidence suggest that the repercussions of a suicide are more profound than I have been able to communicate. If you believe this to be an exaggeration, please err on the side of caution: Postpone your plans and immediately seek crisis intervention. That way, you can buy time to rise to the challenge and research this topic yourself.

Obviously, I cannot talk you out of suicide, but I can show you a way to make a well-informed decision later on. If you are only going to read one book, let it be *Suicide: What Really Happens in the Afterlife?* This extremely well researched book shows time and again that suicides almost always regret their actions soon afterwards. Moreover, unimaginable levels of guilt and remorse haunt them for a long time.[46]

Please consult a professional or research the subject further, both to safeguard your karmic standing and to protect those around you from the profound sorrow and guilt they will feel if you go.

Crime and Punishment

The notion of reward and punishment is deeply embedded within the Judeo-Christian tradition. Accordingly, many of us have a tough time disengaging long enough to consider alternative viewpoints about the consequences of our actions.

When we compare the legal system to spiritual values, we notice tremendous overlaps in the most severe realms. For example, our society imposes daunting penalties for crimes such as terrorism, murder, and sexual predation, to name a few.

On this level, the standards may be nearly identical between man's law and spiritual values, but one wonders how the justice system's penalties jive with the laws of karma. For example, if someone is justifiably convicted of murder and faces life without parole at the age of 25, do her remaining years serve to wipe out her karmic debt, or do they merely make a dent? What about the death penalty? At the time of death, does an executed criminal pay for her crime in full, spiritually? Do executions figure into the collective karma of the society that imposes them? Though I do not have any answers, these are interesting questions to ponder.

Thinking about misdemeanors and low-level felonies is even more intriguing. We all know about shoplifting, moving violations, creating a disturbance, public drunkenness, and so on. However, the pantheon of misdemeanors in the spiritual world may not include all of the ones that are deemed punishable by man-made laws. At the same time, karma encompasses so much more.

Our justice system does not indict for betrayal, backstabbing, malicious gossip, deception, viciousness, lies, empty promises, intimidation, acts of inconsideration, and on and on. So the world of karma encompasses a different set of values and priorities than does our legal system, at least in some cases. Instead of memorizing a list, we can steer our lives in a better direction if we are constantly mindful of "do unto others…."

Remember, spiritual misdemeanors such as controlling others, or indulging in minor abuses of power, predispose us to those situations in the future, when we will be on the receiving end. We may not recognize them as karmic payback because the new circumstances may not remind us of the old, yet the core misdemeanor would be identical. For example, routinely using passive aggression in the workplace may attract a series of passive-aggressive acquaintances later on.

Karma and Prison Life

Let's continue discussing crime and punishment by looking at prison inmates, since incarceration is such an extreme situation. Even though most of us have not experienced imprisonment, we probably think about it from time to time.

One of the most fascinating insights I gained from Martin Scorsese's *Goodfellas* (1990) was that a career criminal might be convicted for the first time, only after his umpteenth offense. He might serve just 10 years for his most recent crime because this is the only one for which he has been apprehended. Some of his other offenses may have been far worse. Spiritually, this is a worthless and short-lived victory for the perpetrator, because legally imposed punishments can fall woefully short of what is due karmically.

Finding God in Prison

Sincerely finding God in prison probably leads to forgiveness from God, but it does not exempt us from the karmic repercussions of our life's actions. Hence, another myth woven into the fabric of our culture is that forgiveness from God wipes the slate clean. Unfortunately, accountability and consequences are as entrenched in the karmic system as gravity is on Earth. Therefore, people in prison for a long time may have only one option for reducing their karmic burden, namely, redemptive acts.

Even within the prison walls, inmates can still help others in a variety of ways. If they have truly found God and have taken full responsibility for all the bad they have generated, they will no doubt experience a radical change in thinking that will prompt them to make positive contributions within their limited environment.

The amount by which their karmic liability decreases will depend upon the size and scope of their overall debt. It will also take into account the motives behind their compassionate acts, the degree of sacrifice involved, and the impact their deeds have on others. Thus, the value of a given act is set in stone, regardless of who initiates it, but the impact on one's karmic standing varies: A purer soul will enjoy a greater karmic reduction than someone with a much heavier load, in terms of percentages.

We can see that even under the most restrictive circumstances, opportunities for both good *and* evil abound. Moreover, free will and the constant need to make decisions—for better and for worse—are as much a part of a prisoner's life as anybody else's. Therefore, when we (non-prisoners) take stock of our current circumstances—however painful, limited, and meager our lives may be—we must acknowledge that we really do have plenty of opportunities for redemptive acts that can lead to karmic debt reduction.

Karma and purpose, along with many other factors, cannot be controlled or easily analyzed. Fortunately, it is a different story with free will, the one spiritual asset we can exercise each and every day, as we will discuss in the next chapter.

Chapter 8

The Law We Consciously Control—Free Will

In the human experience, free will is as omnipresent as water. Regardless of our circumstances or how evolved we are, we can always exercise free will. Even when we face adversity we can still do so, though we may feel like we have a much shorter leash and far fewer options. This is abundantly clear with addicted people who appear to hit rock bottom. Loved ones cannot imagine any option except sobriety, yet, to their astonishment, the addiction sometimes rages on with no end in sight.

Free will is also apparent in our choice to awaken spiritually. For example, for years many people advised me to read Louise Hay's *You Can Heal Your Life*. Deep down I must have known I would have a profound response to this book, because I avoided it for a long time. Once I took the plunge, it turned out to be a major pivotal point and indeed launched my spiritual awakening.

Random Events

Over time, I eventually understood the nature of random events. Regardless of whether we have awakened spiritually or not, our prebirth agenda dictates key events. However, exercising free will in this context can generate substantial results. Indeed, what we make of our lives—in concert with random opportunities and happenings—significantly supplements our spiritual mandates.

All matter is connected, but our ability to make these associations is much greater when we are plugged in spiritually. Furthermore, the quantity and quality of synchronicity (also known as happenstance and serendipity) increases when we are spiritually inclined, while random events decrease.

By exercising free will and consciously *choosing* a spiritual path, we implicitly ask a Higher Power to take over our lives. This always advances our spiritual evolution, but the real-world outcome may not be so wonderful. Moreover, we typically do not comprehend what it *really* means to turn over our lives to a Higher Power.

In the beginning, incredibly good things can happen when we awaken spiritually. This derives from the release of our pent-up spiritual energy, which may have been under wraps for decades. Then we usually enter a period of inactivity, or even stagnation, which can go on for a long time and serves two purposes:

First, this phase is long enough to weed out the insincere. Those motivated solely by thoughts of what they can get out of the real world will probably be discouraged by how long it takes and they may revert to their old ways. I am sure that countless followers of *The Secret* will eventually find themselves at such crossroads.

Second, it provides a probation period of sorts, giving us time to get out if we choose to do so. Once the probation period ends we can still turn back, but we may find such backtracking as tricky as extinguishing our survival instincts, or at least that was my experience with this mysterious phenomenon.

Free Will and Evil

The most evil among us also exercise free will. A hardened and vile criminal can, at any moment, completely turn her life around. To envision the spectrum of good and evil, imagine yet another straight line: At one end is brilliant light; at the other end is pitch-black darkness. We can imagine Saint Teresa at the bright end and Adolph Hitler at the other. The points in between are every possible gradation of gray.

At birth, we are positioned at one end, enveloped by the light. As we get older and understand more of the world, we are frequently presented with opportunities to move away from the light, even with relatively minor decisions. Within this spectrum, every choice we make directs us one way or the other, because any given act is evaluated in relationship to its spiritual implications and our karmic portfolio as a whole.

Osama Bin Laden Had Choices, Too

Osama Bin Laden's situation illustrates some interesting aspects of this discussion. He arrived in Afghanistan with $300 million.[47] After Afghanistan's war with Russia, Bin Laden had some clear choices: Instead of setting up terrorist training camps, he could have helped the Afghanis by supplying them with food and medicine. Since the Bin Laden family's $5 billion fortune came from construction, he also could have enlisted some Saudis to help the Afghanis rebuild.[48] Even if he insisted that they call him King Osama, this would have been a miniscule transgression compared to what he actually did: He made generous donations to local charities and paid off the Taliban to ensure that he could run terrorist training camps without interference. The rest is history. This story can be used to demonstrate several important spiritual principles:

One, we will eventually judge ourselves in relation to the circumstances and resources that were at hand when we made a given choice. In Bin Laden's case, he squandered his formidable assets on executing an evil plan instead of relieving the overwhelming needs of the Afghanis.

Two, any evil deed produces severely intensified spiritual consequences when it is enacted in the name of God.

Three, motives can be almost as important as the impact on others, especially in this case. Bin Laden contributed to local charities, but he was motivated by gaining support for his safe haven rather than by a sincere desire to help the Afghanis. The favorable spiritual results of his philanthropy were virtually wiped out by his nefarious motive.

Free Will and the Average Person's Philanthropy

In a vaguely similar vein, this reminds me of people who believe that charitable donations ensure a ticket to Heaven or of business executives who decide how much they will allocate to charity based on the optimal impact on their tax liability. Again, the motive degrades the potency of the generosity, but far less than in the Bin Laden example.

The same applies to the so-called "tenfold" principle. Some people believe that whatever they give away will eventually come back to them 10 times more than the original amount. This belief surely diminishes that possibility because our motive is tied into what we can get out of it.

The highest octave of philanthropy presupposes giving without expectations of reward. Whatever the motivation, this all plays out on the spiritual plane for better and for worse.

Lightness, Darkness, and Restitution

Let's return to that straight line, with brilliant light at one end and blackness at the other. As previously mentioned, each choice can move us in one direction or another.

Twelve-step programs implicitly address this with their emphasis on making amends. Not only can addicts ruin their own lives, but they can also wreak havoc upon the lives of others, creating both profoundly negative karma and a slippery slide towards darkness until they clean up their act. Making amends through heartfelt apologies and/or restitution can make an impressive difference in both cases.

In making amends, the impact on our spiritual lives is relative to the amount of sacrifice involved. Consider a recovering addict who decides to initiate a restitution program for the financial damage he has done to others. He figures out how much he owes and to whom. He then divides a monthly sum among these people and makes regular payments until they are repaid in full.

In spiritual terms, this would go a long way towards paying off karma and moving closer to the light. Not only does it acknowledge the negative impact of this person's previous actions, but the motives are pure because this addict expects nothing more than to make restitution and wipe the financial slate clean. We do not have to be addicts or participate in a 12-step program to try this sort of restitution ourselves. What we have learned here is that the more self-serving the motive, the less it counts spiritually.

The Light-Dark Accumulation Effect

When we are in either a move-to-the-light or move-to-the-dark mode, we might experience an avalanche effect. Sometimes, the more we move in one direction, the more we feel compelled to continue in that direction.

Some of us, consciously or unwittingly, slip and slide into a dark chasm. If and when we respond to a wake-up call, we usually allow specific goals to guide us back into lighter territory. For example, we might want to return to the stability we once enjoyed. However, the climb back up can be difficult and discouraging because we must travel back through the darkness towards the light.

For most of us, our daily choices represent a mix of spiritual misdemeanors and mild mitigations. If we lean in one direction more than the other, our movement along that path may still be nearly imperceptible in the short term. However, over time our position within a given sphere will become far more obvious. For example, a judging or controlling woman may become so locked into this behavior that these characteristics, which may have been less noticeable in her 30s, are perceived as her dominant personality traits when the woman is in her 50s. Of course, we can always change, but offensive habits are far more ingrained and much harder to detect, the longer we practice them. In these instances, a spiritual awakening–followed by a sincere willingness to learn lessons–may be the only way back to a lighter realm.

Free Will and the Unconscious

Our unconscious words and actions also have an impact on the spiritual plane, but they involve a different set of rules. Here, too, we have the spectrum of light and darkness, but it relates to how aware or unconscious we are. We are all responsible for our decisions and actions, regardless of their source. A vicious act generated by the unconscious is still vile and subject to karmic ramifications, even if some messed-up motive in our unconscious could be the driving force behind it.

For example, in the past my arrogance and complete lack of compassion prompted me to belittle people from time to time. Each instance would negatively impact my karmic standing, yet I continued to thrive in darkness regarding this issue. Decades later I developed empathy and the arrogance has all but completely evaporated. Today, my altered consciousness allows me to see what I once did to people and I can no longer justify such insensitivities.

As far as the good/evil spectrum goes, the best I can do now is to handle similar situations with greater tact and compassion, which will eventually push me towards the light a smidge at a time. I believe I must break even—by accumulating as many compassionate acts as there were inconsiderate and deprecating ones—before I actually move forward into new karmic territory.

In this situation, spiritual restitution operates in the background. Once I cast off the arrogance and gained compassion, my newfound understanding made me consciously choose to act responsibly in similar situations. When I abide by these perceptions, I am in sync with my consciousness. If I should ever revert back to my old ways, I would do so with a rehabilitated consciousness. Therefore, that would be an even more serious transgression than the original, when all this stuff was still unconscious, because I truly know what I am doing now.

When an act is ruled by the unconscious, we are never excused for the impact it has on others. However, the degree of karmic agitation is somewhat less severe than if the offense involved a willful and consciously informed decision.

Free Will, Duality, and Theodicy

Not only is free will a given, but the dual nature of our collective reality constantly presents itself in myriad forms. These opposites include good and evil, passive and active, visible and invisible, audible and silent, and so on. Free will figures in when we must decide between black-and-white opposites, or, more typically, among the gray points in between.

Theodicy—the Catholic study of suffering, fairness/justice, and free will in mystical terms—proposes that the paramount function of free will refers to intentionally choosing a life infused with spiritual meaning. If life were fair, we would routinely be rewarded for good acts and punished for bad ones. However, the sooner we realize that life is all too often unjust, the better.

If we open our eyes, we will eventually observe that evil people get away with plenty of transgressions and serious crimes, while it sometimes seems like "no good deed goes unpunished." These particular facts of life both annoy and mystify us. However, if we really think about it, we will realize that every time we choose to act out of benevolence, we also decide to acknowledge someone else's need.

Self-interest drives us in many different ways and is not always a bad thing. Still, it is a given that influences most of our decisions. Hence, if we were always rewarded and punished *fairly*, then the promise of advancement coupled with the threat of recrimination would become the compelling forces behind all of our actions. The Pavlovian principle would then be our foremost inspiration.

Without guaranteed results, our good actions have far more meaning and value, because we are not doing them for compensation. In the big picture, we can assume that God wants us to opt for Him through free will alone. Incentives dilute the power of this choice.

Similarly, when we are in the early stages of a relationship, we want someone who will accept us as we are, rather than a potential partner who is only lured in by our looks, bank account, or connections. Consequently, attractive, wealthy, and powerful people often experience great uncertainty when they welcome new people into their lives. They have to sort through all kinds of signals to get to the heart of the other person's true motives.

Conversely, "trophy" relationships involve two parties who are trading off one another's superficial assets, so the mutual rewards are built into their respective decisions.

God does not want millions of trophies, but rather the real deal, one earnest volunteer at a time. Surely, we present ourselves to God as potential trophies when the law of attraction prompts us to demand: "Give me this. Give me that."

When we opt for a spiritually motivated life, we sometimes unleash the terms of our prebirth agenda for the first time. As we have discussed many times thus far, this frequently means attracting undesirable experiences that serve as the forum for lessons we agreed to learn. If these unpleasant events do not sway us from our own spirituality, then our commitment is enriched.

The Challenges of Tremendous Loss

Tremendous losses make some of us feel like we are being tested by God, or that the loss is strong evidence that God does not exist.

I am reminded of Taylor, who lost his child to leukemia. This particular trial was far greater than most of us could withstand, so it was no surprise that Taylor's anger towards God developed into a full-blown rejection. God does not penalize people in such cases because conscious acknowledgment of God is not a prerequisite for spiritual progress. Rather, the choices Taylor makes after the initial grieving period are far more important. The key questions to consider are:

- Did Taylor transform his grief into something positive? Did something good eventually emerge from this tragic loss?
- Did the bereavement turn Taylor so sour that his relationships with others suffered as a result?
- Did Taylor cling to the mourning long after the healing should have started?
- Did his attitude and behavior deteriorate, or did Taylor maintain the level of kindness, etc. that he possessed before his child got sick?
- Despite the overwhelming sorrow, did Taylor get through life one day at a time, or was he merely an empty shell?

In this example, we can see how free will figures into even our greatest hardships and how rejecting God means nothing as long as it does not adversely influence the decisions we make and who we are at our core.

Religion and Mysticism

Though the Vatican continues to offer mysticism in the form of Theodicy to seminary students, rank-and-file Catholics do not have easy access to these writings.‡ Likewise, the other major religions spend little, if any, time discussing such matters. They seem to think that such exchanges should be reserved for one-on-one consultations with religious clerics, such as mullahs, monks, and ministers.

As part of Jewish mysticism, ancient Kabbalah writings have become popular in the past 20 years, but that seems to be the extent of mysticism in the mainstream. Though organized religions do offer some other benefits, their general refusal to highlight mystical elements—including helpful discussions about free will and suffering—weakens their potential as laudable spiritual guides. Our discussion of religion in other contexts sheds more light on this topic, as we shall see in the next chapter.

‡ Luckily, the kind people at St. Barnard's Seminary in Rochester, NY allowed me to research there for a few weeks in 1993.

Part 3
Universal Laws and Spiritual Issues

Taoists: Shit happens.
Hindus: This shit happened before.
Catholics: If shit happens, you deserve it.
Jews: Why does shit always happen to us?
Protestants: Let shit happen to someone else.
Buddhists: If shit happens, it is not really shit.
Christian Evangelists on TV: Send more shit.
Zen Buddhists: What is the sound of shit happening?
Atheists: No shit.[49]

Chapter 9

Religion, Spirituality and Prayers

World religions share a few things in common: One way or another, most religious leaders tell their followers that regular attendance at their place of worship goes a long way towards salvation. They also convey the message that specific beliefs and rituals—along with strict adherence to scriptures—are necessary to maintain a strong relationship with God.

Comparing Scriptures

Comparing scriptures from the oldest and most prevalent religions reveals unexpectedly strong connections among them. In Los Angeles during the early 1990s, I attended an impromptu lecture in Griffith Park. A comparative religions professor talked about inputting all the scriptures into a computer in such a way that all the beliefs and directives would be abbreviated in a standard format. Then, at the push of a button, all the matching philosophies would be deleted to see what was left.

According to this teacher, the overlaps would be greater than 90 percent, leaving only 10 percent of the content that was not mirrored by all other religions. Within that 10 percent, identical matches still occurred among some of the doctrines. Eliminating these, we would then be left with only a few unique philosophies that appear in one religion and none of the others. This teacher claimed that these stand-alone elements would not necessarily be offensive to the religions that appeared to have overlooked these issues.[§]

I found this to be a stunning claim at first, but after careful deliberation I understood what was not immediately apparent: It boils down to what is highlighted versus what is put on the back burner. For example, Buddhism places heavy emphasis on the many facets of suffering and compassion, although we do not hear as much about these issues from the other religions. In this instance, I could not think of any doctrine that would argue with the Buddhist position. The other religions simply place their priorities elsewhere. Similarly, religions that value the 10 commandments would be hard pressed to find opposing sentiments from other faiths.

This discussion reminds me of the differences among 24-hour cable news channels. If we factor in the information crawling along the bottom of the screen, the variations narrow considerably, especially when we bear in mind their respective political differences. For example, a liberal newscast might devote a few minutes every hour to a specific story for an entire day, while its conservative counterpart reduces the same story to one sentence, which appears in their crawl for only 12 hours. However, both networks are covering the story. One is simply emphasizing it more than the other. From this discussion, we can deduce that:

- No one religion holds the patent on the truth
- Multiple religions exist to give everyone a choice
- We can infer a connection among all religious followers due to the striking similarities among their respective scriptures
- If we are dissatisfied with our current religion, we really should feel free to experiment elsewhere.

---

§ Unfortunately, I did not take note of this insightful man's name.

The Pluses and Minuses of Organized Religion

Under the most favorable circumstances, religions offer some good things to regular attendees, including:

- A way to check our moral navigation systems based on messages from the pulpit
- A place to go once a week to focus on spiritual matters
- Opportunities to serve the community
- A fellowship of like-minded people.

Unfortunately, any given place of worship is subject to the strengths and weaknesses of its current leadership. Even though the values and attitudes expressed may suit most followers, it may not be the best place for all of them. Furthermore, within any given American religion, the regional distinctions are sometimes quite remarkable. Subtle or sometimes blatant cultural differences, coupled with the mindsets of the preachers. make all the difference. For example, one locality might be quite conservative and literal in terms of scripture, while another is tolerant, progressive, and more creative in its interpretations, yet they both operate under the same banner.

If religion seems to be the best way to approach spirituality, then we owe it to ourselves to branch out and try new things. The most compelling reason to do so is the deafness we sometimes acquire about familiar concepts, which can eventually reduce then to no more than a broken record. The messages we are desperate to hear—at least unconsciously— may only be perceived within a fresh and unconventional context. This is the main reason that I have dabbled as much as I have in comparative religions. I do not find that any given faith has all the answers, but among them I find a wealth of possibilities. The so-called "cafeteria approach" to spiritual information works best for me—a little bit of this and a little bit of that.

Krishnamurti and the Order of the Star

The story of Jiddu Krishnamurti's (1895-1986) involvement with a popular religion of his time allows us to see religion from another distinct perspective.

In 1909, an elder of the Theosophy movement spotted the 13-year-old Krishnamurti on a beach in India. Captivated by the boy's selfless aura, the man thought Krishnamurti could be the leader that the Theosophists had been seeking for their yet-to-be-formed religion, The Order of the Star. After years of grooming and education in both India and England, Krishnamurti grew up to be gifted beyond the elders' wildest expectations. By the summer of 1929, The Order of the Star was thriving with 60,000 followers and an impressive list of assets, including plenty of cash and real estate.[50]

Moreover, Krishnamurti continued to dazzle his followers. Therefore, it came as quite a shock when Krishnamurti disbanded The Order of the Star in August 1929. During his dissolution speech, Krishnamurti introduced various arguments against organized religions and these theories continued as the basis of his lectures for many decades thereafter.

In essence, Krishnamurti claimed that many paths lead to the truth, but that no leaders should take us there. The structure of an organized religion—coupled with the human limitations of any leader—generates a reduction and an over-simplification of spiritual matters. Organized religions, he said, are essentially counterproductive because the truth must be aspired to, not handed down in a diluted form. We must sincerely seek the truth and be internally driven to ever-higher precipices. We must be proactive, not passive. We must be self-reliant, not dependent on others for viewpoints that simply rub off on us.[51]

Krishnamurti was also concerned with the mandate espoused by organized religions. Followers who buy into this presumed authority are trapping themselves within the confines of that religion. In other words, the doctrines of any given religion become set in stone and do not leave room for individual differences, particularly the subtle level of spiritual development that exists in one person at any given time. Therefore, organized religions can, ironically, stunt the growth of their followers, according to Krishnamurti. [52]

Regarding my own spiritual health, I wholeheartedly agree with Krishnamurti. Shortly after my spiritual awakening, Krishnamurti's ideas became self-evident, though I had not heard of him at the time. I had the strongest feeling that organized religions had very little to do with spirituality.

Nevertheless, I cannot disparage organized religions to quite the extent that Krishnamurti did. I believe that for some people organized religions serve as necessary stepping-stones to awakening. Because certain religions permeate our culture, subscribing to them offers some rewards, as outlined earlier in this chapter.

Those of us who value our involvement in a religion might want to take stock of the features we deem important. On the highest end, we might value the fellowship and the opportunities to serve the community. On the lowest end, we may regularly attend a place of worship simply because community pressures force us to. The real question is: How much does this religion contribute to our spiritual evolution?

Free will and preparedness must be factored in as well. Krishnamurti's philosophy may not appeal to those who have yet to awaken spiritually. Similarly, those with a contrary opinion may block out Krishnamurti's radical proposals, or they may feel comfortable staying dependent on religious leadership. Under the best possible circumstances, religion may do no harm, but regular worship could postpone a spiritual awakening if our attendance is not supplemented by spiritually driven awareness and behavior.

The only way a religion can actually corrode a person's soul is through the arrogance of exclusionist, condemnatory, and spiritually truncating doctrine: "Our way is the only way," or, "those who believe X, Y, and Z are the only ones who will find salvation." This approach is inherently dangerous and most certainly anti-spiritual because it:

- Creates a sense of smugness and righteousness that is so pronounced at times that it is downright offensive and always spiritually counter-productive

- Nurtures attitudes and behaviors that negate the possibility of significant, authentic spiritual growth
- Almost always leads to proselytizing, which drives non-believers crazy. If only proselytizers knew how much their bullying pushes people in the opposite direction
- Inferentially annihilates other paths and effectively states that non-believers are doomed to Hell
- Detaches the group's followers from the rest of the world, positioning them on a very low spiritual echelon. Acknowledging the interconnections of all beings is so basic to spiritual growth that it comes soon after a spiritual awakening and long before the slightest inkling of enlightenment.

Nevertheless, we are here to fulfill our prebirth agendas and our beliefs fall outside this mandate. Just like everyone else, churchgoers run the gamut of virtue from generous to stingy, selfless to selfish, sincere to hypocritical, arrogant to self-effacing, etc.

Finally, I do believe that followers of an organized religion can advance spiritually, but their progress is most often catalyzed by circumstances *outside* the church's framework. Of course, such advancement occurs far less often to diehard supporters of our-way-or-the-highway dogmas.

Whether we subscribe to an organized religion or not, virtually all people who believe in God have dabbled in prayer at one time or another.

Unanswered Prayers

As we discussed earlier, asking God for help takes many different forms, such as prayers, chants, visualizations, incantations, affirmations, and so on.

The first things to consider are both the underlying motives and the tenor of our petitions. Hence, we must ask ourselves several questions:

- Are we a sincere adult, or a child on the verge of a tantrum, as I was with 12 pages of demands for a better material life?
- Do our requests refer more to our desire to grow or to our sense of entitlement?
- Do our appeals in any way imply harm to others?
- Do we fully comprehend that most petitions are heard but not answered?

Unfortunately, my own situation and observations of others prove this last point to be true. The mechanism at work allows resolution only for circumstances that do not interfere with our spiritual mandate. The story told earlier about the toddler and the mattress illustrates the inner workings of miracles and explains why, against all odds, some prayers may be answered in an apparently spectacular fashion.

However, if we widen our definition of "miracle" to include unexpected solutions to niggling situations, we then see that a miracle can help us without interfering with our spiritual blueprint. For example, I remember a 60-something woman named Gina whose son supplemented her social security with a monthly stipend of $200. Gina was able to make ends meet until her son lost his job due to a serious, chronic medical condition.

Three weeks later, her next-door neighbor asked if Gina would consider renting out the room above her garage to his sister. This room was being used for storage at the time. Gina said that she would, but the room needed to be cleared out, painted, and furnished. Her neighbor offered to do all of that for free. In addition, the sister said she could only pay $400/month, but she was willing to clean Gina's house every week, mow the lawn, and shovel the snow.

We see these kinds of miracles every day and they all share two common features: Out of the blue, a situation arises that converts pain into comfort. At the same time, the new circumstances never interfere with our spiritual agenda. Otherwise, they would remain unanswered prayers.

Nothing stops us from petitioning God, but we must focus on the ends rather than the means. For example, I am a lottery addict, forever on the verge of recovery. I do not really spend a lot of money on the lottery; rather, I squander too much time believing I am going to win and dreaming about the trip to lotto headquarters.

Praying to the Lottery Gods

My lotto fantasies date back to the 1970s. At that time, I would condo shop *before* the drawing and it went rapidly downhill from there. I used to (half-) jokingly say that the lottery gods "must be really backlogged and they will get to me next time." So I have a sorry history of frittering away a lot of thought and energy on something that has not materialized and probably never will despite years on end of practicing affirmations according to the law of attraction.

Those of us who have not read *The Secret* probably found the last story a bit harebrained. However, *The Secret* features a few similar gems here and there, written by some of its 24 contributors. Of course, the comparable, goofy stories recounted in *The Secret* produced a full manifestation of whatever had been desired. Therefore, I should have won $10 million many times over by now, according to *The Secret*. In any case, a steadfast belief in the law of attraction predisposes some devotees to temporarily abandon their good sense so they can pursue monumental dreams.

Since I never won the lottery, let's return to what actually happened.

In 2001, I was dead broke because my part-time job simply did not cover even the basics. Then I heard a line in a movie that went something like this: "Sometimes we have to let a dream go to make room for a miracle." This became a major epiphany, especially when I connected it to my lottery obsession. I realized that we can focus on an end, but we must allow the Universe to provide the means. If we tresspass on that territory, we effectively close off all other channels through which the Universe might operate, so we stay stuck in limbo. In this state of stagnation, absolutely nothing happens in terms of advancing our goals.

By connecting the dots, I realized that if I discontinued the lottery I would probably abort all the scheming that went along with it. The next day, I still felt compelled to walk away from this obsession, and of course, I had not increased my net worth by even a dime in those 24 hours. Astonishingly, my boss then offered me new duties that would double my hours within a few months.

The lesson here was not to stop playing the lotto, but to consider dropping counterproductive habits and thoughts. In my case, the increased hours meant ascending the economic ladder from destitution to a hand-to-mouth state. Evidently, *my* Divine plan did not call for buckets of cash to arrive via another opportunity at that time. I had no choice but to trust that such financial constraints served a spiritual purpose. I also had to confront the possibility that I might never acquire the wealth I so clearly envisioned, because it might be forever at odds with my spiritual agenda. (As a side note, I still buy lottery tickets, but my investments to date remain far greater than the paltry winnings I have accumulated. The good news is that I spend a lot less time thinking about it.)

Is God Deaf?

When we are enveloped by circumstances that defy the fulfillment of our goals, we have sometimes been sidetracked so we can learn lessons or pay off karma. At other times, we may be unwittingly serving a purpose that we would not have agreed to pursue if we had known the particulars. These periods can span months, or even years, while we keep trying to set ourselves free from the adversity, to no avail. However, the more failed escape attempts we accumulate, the more likely Divine sources are at work in accordance with the prebirth contract we signed.

When we evaluate a past period of adversity, we rarely can distinguish among lessons, karma, or purpose, but we may retroactively understand that these hardships paved the way to some sort of spiritual improvement. The growth would not have been possible without the painful contrast between our desires and the experience of receiving *anything but* the means to achieve them. My own experiences and observations tell me how true this is, but *The Secret's* dominant theme runs counter to this important point.[53]

Sincere spiritual seekers may or may not incorporate spiritual practices and petitions to God into their daily lives, but they usually seek enlightenment, as we will discuss in the next chapter.

Chapter 10
Enlightenment and Consciousness

Prayer sometimes leads to enlightenment because our petitions make us alert and ready for direction, both from within ourselves and from outside sources. Of course, enlightenment does not occur all at once. Rather, our consciousness expands a little bit with each epiphany.

Some people are not consciously plugged in spiritually, but mellow over the years anyway. These individuals experience dozens of epiphanies through lessons learned and absorb them into their psyche in small fragments. Therefore, we do not have to be spiritually attuned to benefit from consciousness expansion.

Can We Measure Enlightenment?

The progression of enlightenment is similar to going from complete blindness to 20/20 vision with thousands of increments along the way. If we observe a huge spiritual leap forward, we simply cannot gauge its relative value: We cannot figure out where on the spectrum we began and how many steps we have just taken. Thus, enlightenment is measured in degrees, yet it cannot be quantified.[❡]

❡ This discussion of enlightenment is metaphysically inspired and only refers to the Buddhist perspective in a tangential fashion.

Unfortunately, we are only as perceptive as our spiritual maturity allows. Therefore, what *seems* like a giant step could be just that or it could turn out to be much smaller, when observed within the larger scheme of things. In a given area, we can advance from totally blind to barely seeing anything and remain in that state for eons.

The Tranquilized Turtle

Our movement towards clarity is barely perceptible within a given lifetime, but impressive growth spurts are possible. In fact, some people enjoy the rare privilege of a spillover effect: When one facet undergoes a successful overhaul, it sometimes trickles down to favorably influence other areas.

More typically, we leisurely zigzag through life like a turtle on tranquilizers. Then again, the animal is sedated, so sleeping takes up most of its time. Once in a blue moon, the turtle overdoses on espresso and scurries along. At such times, the creature covers a lot of ground in a short period, only to fall asleep again.

Epiphanies

These jolts often produce epiphanies, or translucent moments when we say, "Aha!" And they characteristically herald a spiritual advance. In these moments of clarity, we discover a truth as finally self-evident. We also comprehend that right now must be the time when we are most receptive to this knowledge, in a way not possible before.

Epiphanies and Addiction

These epiphanies could activate the turning point in healing an addiction. For example, let's look at Cassandra, an alcoholic mother of two who lost her job due to excessive absences. She was simply too hung over to make it to work every day. Cassandra liked her job and getting fired was a serious financial blow. For her, this was a wakeup call, permitting her to see the writing on the wall.

Cassandra took stock and accurately projected that if she continued drinking she could lose everything, including her kids. Until this time, Cassandra had been completely in denial, but losing her job shocked her into reality.

I have seen this happen several times with dramatic results. Not only does the addict in recovery heal the main cause for concern, such as job retention, but many other things also fall effortlessly into place, as if the substance abuse had impaired almost every facet of this person's life in ways not obvious to the observer, let alone to the addict.

We have already discussed the slow road back from darkness for most addicts, but for some reason a few people enjoy a rapid recovery. This phenomenon usually mystifies loved ones as much as it does the recovering addict.

Transporting Wisdom from One Life to Another

Another variable entails the state of spiritual development we carry from one life to the next. In the afterlife, we may or may not take the opportunity to learn more and thus develop beyond the level we occupied at death. Either way, we do not lose ground when we reincarnate, but it might take some of us until our late 30s (or even later) to resurrect our true evolutionary status. Conversely, we sometimes see pre-adolescent children who show an astounding spiritual comprehension, but they are rare birds indeed.

One Hurdle at a Time

We can be incredibly evolved in some areas, yet still remain quite primitive in others. One spiritual leap does not necessarily influence other areas in need of healing. For example, when we start to understand the interconnectivity of all things, we may become more helpful. Perhaps we volunteer for the first time ever, or we look out for people who seem to need our assistance. Over time, our unabated growth may enhance our generosity in ways we never thought possible. Yet, we may still find forgiveness in a particular situation untenable, or we may even find ourselves preoccupied with jealousy and envy from time to time.

Let's now explore a few myths associated with enlightenment:

Myth: Consuming Large Quantities of Metaphysical Material Promotes Spiritual Expansion

Attending lectures, reading books, and listening to audiotapes generate many rewards, to be sure. We definitely can enrich our lives as follows:

First, we often feel centered and reassured.

Second, our understanding of one or more spiritual facets may evolve from dim to translucent.

Third, we can reconfigure our place in the scheme of things and possibly adjust our understanding of spiritual matters in a significant manner.

Fourth, we may be able to better distinguish between our spiritual and physical lives. This could add new meaning to our words and actions and promote a deeper understanding of the link between how we conduct our lives on Earth and the impact this has on our spiritual well-being. These types of changes can be very subtle, but their effects build up over time. In fact, it is possible to accumulate enough of these to eventually reach critical mass, which in turn instigates a meaningful transformation. Despite its power, the whole process takes place outside conscious awareness.

Fifth, our values may be altered to some degree, which beneficially influences behaviors and decisions. As a rule, only highly perceptive people can identify these nuances, but they also accumulate. The rest of us, including myself, usually recognize these subtleties in hindsight after enough time has passed to accrue several examples of the new values in action.

Nevertheless, no spiritual advances can be made unless our fresh insights are *followed by actions* that reflect the new information. We always hear that "knowledge is power," but in the end, knowledge is merely an intellectual achievement unless we do something with it.

We sometimes accumulate so much knowledge that we come to a

favorable breaking point. The scales tip. The time is right. And after a very long phase of apparent stagnation, inspiration leads us to the best course of action. This is particularly true for people who have successfully overcome addiction to the point that they are no longer hounded by thoughts of their previous substances of choice. To achieve this, one must dig deep to pinpoint the unconscious triggers and redirect an assortment of anxieties away from the addiction towards a constructive outlet.

Myth: Philanthropy, Volunteering, and Doing Things for Others Guarantee a Ticket to Heaven

So many religions insidiously endorse this standpoint that it is endemic in our culture. Promoters of this doctrine rarely examine the intricacies of our actions' spiritual implications. I talk at length elsewhere in this book about karma as well as philanthropy and they come into play here as well.

Within the karmic context, the value of all actions is influenced by our motives, the impact on others, and the degree of sacrifice involved on our part. If we are driven by the ticket-to-Heaven mentality, we are devaluing our generous actions to an extent. In this case, we get a credit in our karmic bank account, but we may be paid back through a good deed generated by another person with the same thinking. Of course, this is a good thing, but it is a far cry from a trumpeted welcome at the pearly gates.

If we are stuck in this thinking, one mitigating factor is how great the impact is on another person. For example, if we give $25 to an employed person, the effect is less profound than if we give it to a homeless individual. Similarly, if we give away our *last* $25, this entails a marked level of sacrifice that does not apply if we enjoy a healthy net worth. Finally, if we are primarily motivated to give so we can impress a new love interest, then we significantly diminish the potentially good karma. The generosity is still worth something, but it is now valued much lower than the kind of philanthropy that is devoid of self-interest.

Myth: If Only I Could Spend the Rest of My Life in a Himalayan Cave

At some point on our journey to accumulate spiritual knowledge, some of us find ourselves in the first or second grade, having graduated with honors from kindergarten. At this juncture, a little bit of knowledge can lead us to mistakenly believe certain things that are way off the mark. For example, some of us think that having the means to spend the rest of our lives hopping from one self-help/metaphysical lecture to another around the country, or living for years in an ashram will guarantee enlightenment in a way not otherwise possible. Check out two reasons why this is not true:

One, if either of these scenarios were implanted into our spiritual agenda, the appropriate opportunities would eventually arise and everything would fall into place to make one of them happen.

Two, we were born into our current reality for a reason and it is unrelated to these ascetic fantasies. Therefore, 99.9 percent of us are meant to grow and change based on the very circumstances in our lives, right here, right now.

If this proposition seems unappealing, please consider the following: We incorrectly conclude that accruing knowledge cures what ails us and leads to Nirvana in one form or another. Truthfully, these kinds of fantasies are similar to wanting to be a beach bum who endlessly surfs and pursues creative endeavors. They all amount to escapism of the highest order. However, fantasies like these are harmless enough as long as we acknowledge them as whimsy and dismiss them as such. The danger comes when we believe that attaining these goals for real would truly solve our adversities.

Furthermore, if we do acquire the means to actually live out these dreams, we will soon discover that peace of mind may be just as elusive in our idealized world as it was before. In our escapism, we are resisting the lessons implied by either our hardship or our desire to abandon an exasperating person or situation. Spiritual liberation depends upon dealing with these circumstances and running away achieves nothing except to put our spiritual development on hold. Remember, whatever we have not addressed in one lifetime comes back intact the next time around.

We can only release our demons within our everyday existence in a very practical and earthly fashion. The earnest spiritual seeker is obligated to make the best of a bad situation and navigate through life as best she can. A sincere pursuit yields many more positive results down the road, even when the darkness makes it impossible to believe this could be so.

Individual and Collective Consciousnesses

Let's now distinguish between cultural influences and individuals within a given environment. No matter where we live in the world, we may find other cultures alien and even distasteful. One lesson intended for everyone is the challenge to increase our tolerance and recognize that everybody is here for similar spiritual reasons, regardless of their citizenship or religious preference.

When we evaluate a given government, we must differentiate between prevailing politics and the people they represent. For example, disturbing actions by Saddam Hussein never reflected the sensibility of most Iraqi people. So our lesson here is to always make this distinction.

We cannot evaluate a dysfunctional culture by indicting the collective. Rather, the lights have to go on at the rate of one person at a time, spreading slowly throughout the group. If we doubt the effectiveness of this, just look at what Mothers Against Drunk Driving (MADD) has done. It took one woman who lost a child to a drunk driver to completely revolutionize our culture. Prior to MADD's inception, our drunk-driving laws failed to adequately acknowledge the connection between blood-alcohol levels and serious accidents. One by one, the lights went on and a culture—once somewhat indulgent of drunk drivers—became completely intolerant.

This discussion of the collective may seem daunting, but in the end only two issues count: Personal reflection and action. If we want cultural healing, we as individuals must evolve. As spiritual entities on Earth, our culture is as much embedded into our psyche as our past personal lives. Hence, our responsibility within the collective is to identify issues we feel need healing and to work on them within our own lives. As more and more people set the example, we may eventually see constructive and even drastic changes.

We can use recycling as an example. In-depth environmental efforts in Northern California have been widespread for so long that recycling is now rooted in that region's culture. In some other areas of America, recycling is at the same stage as it was in Northern California in the 1980s. If this is important to those of us who live in one of these areas, we can upgrade our own personal standards as well as get involved locally.

Hence, we are only asked to honor our own standards and ethics, which we can do by having our actions and attitudes mirror them. We do not have to become a political activist or an aggressor. This can all be done quietly at the appropriate time. The MADD and Northern California examples demonstrate how contagious realigned thinking can be.

So far in this chapter, we have examined enlightenment and consciousness from a number of unusual perspectives. In the next two sections, we will expand the discussion of consciousness much further. The next segment illustrates our own limited understanding of cosmic theories, based on our inability to activate the mind's vast, dormant sector.

Light Bulbs and Lasers

Physicist David Bohm uses the hologram as an analogy to bridge the gap between knowable and unknowable phenomena. The holographic plate (from which a hologram is made) looks much like an underexposed photo negative when viewed under ordinary light. However, when we direct a laser onto the plate, it looks like an open window. Just as with a real window, the entire scene beyond becomes visible through any part of the window.[54]

If the hologram only comes to life with laser power, we surely live in a light bulb world with the complexities and secrets contained in the hologram unavailable to us. Everything in what we call the real world is intrinsically limited.

Animals and Humans

Observing animals makes me understand this completely. I once knew a bulldog named Hugo, who went to the vet for shots and fainted when he saw the needle. By the time his next shots were due, Hugo had apparently forgotten about his last visit to the vet, because he sat quietly in the waiting room minding his own business. Then a door opened and out came a woman in a lab coat. Hugo took one look at her and passed out again.

Let's imagine what Hugo might have been thinking when he woke up: "Why would my otherwise doting owner put me through such torture?" and "What good could possibly come from a stabbing?" If Hugo's owner could hear these questions, she would of course want to tell him about all the benefits of getting annual shots and that a needle jab is a small price to pay relative to the protection the shots offer.

Of course, this exchange could never take place because Hugo's brain could never comprehend its meaning even if he understood the words. Therefore, Hugo's brain is like the 10 percent of our mind that functions fully on Earth. Only when we trigger the other 90 percent do we begin to understand the whys and wherefores of our own adversity as well as the countless intricacies of how everything works together.

Similarly, when we find ourselves in an unpalatable situation, we cannot blatantly call on God and hope He makes an appearance in our living room to explain what is going on here. Like the dog, we do not have the capacity to understand, even if an explanation would emerge. Author Robert Ornstein elaborates:

> Our senses are as selective as cats' whiskers; our eyes focus on a small spot within the radiant electro-magnetic band; our ears respond to a narrow bandwidth of mechanical waves. Very little of the available

information passes the barrier into our "known" world.

Robert Ornstein
The Mind Field

Nevertheless, we do experience subtle bandwidth expansions, even within our limited consciousness on Earth, as we will see in the next section.

Bandwidth

When we study spiritual material, a concept that makes no sense for a long time may become crystal clear years later. This involves a bandwidth shift within our consciousness. It is similar to the taste bud maturation we experience as adults. Junk foods appeal to children, who tend to rebuff healthier options. Yet, adults often enjoy foods they rejected in childhood. Similarly, as our consciousness evolves, our ability to understand and appreciate more advanced concepts also increases.

Therefore, no material is bad, per se. If it speaks to us at the time we are reading it, then it matches our current state of receptivity. If it seems almost like it is written in a foreign language, then our consciousness is not welcoming at this point.

I have observed that so-called "inspirational" material—the kind that soothes the reader—is extremely popular, which confirms the idea that we live in a culture hungry for comfort. This is the dominant motif now and it can be seen in the ever-increasing waistlines of the American population as well as in the persistence of drug abuse and alcoholism. We seek comfort at all costs and some of us pay a very high price for it.

The bottom line here is that we must not overvalue the spiritual understandings we accumulate. By and large, reading books, listening to audiotapes, etc. are strictly cerebral exercises. We must not be fooled into thinking that accumulating a massive bibliography makes us more spiritual or that it gives us an edge over less informed individuals. The truth is that some people who have no intellectual understanding of spirituality may be leading far more spiritually enriched lives than those who read lots of spiritual books or who are deeply entrenched in one religion or another. This means that an individual's actions and attitudes carry far more weight—for better and for worse—than the most astounding metaphysical writings or the most striking lectures from the pulpit. Indeed, we all know plenty of avid spiritual readers and devout churchgoers whose lives are messed up to one degree or another.

Nevertheless, two things can be done to speed up the process:

The first entails taking stock of our lives on a regular basis, matching up various situations with our newly acquired awareness. This is a simple exercise, but I know first-hand that it is never easy. Much of our junk in the attic, so to speak, cannot be easily discerned and discarded, because it is deeply buried in our subconscious.

Consequently, the second strategy permits petitions to God for greater clarity. True, we must tread carefully with prayers, affirmations, etc, because we never know what the Universe will send us. Nevertheless, "Show me the way to greater understanding" should work in this case. We will take a small risk in the short term, but we should eventually harvest the illumination we are seeking.

One of *The Secret's* greatest failures is its trivialization of the issues proposed in this chapter. Our egos respond to *The Secret's* promises of instant gratification but, over time, devotees of *The Secret* will find themselves shortchanged and disappointed in the real world. Furthermore, they will have suspended or even stunted their spiritual growth and may waste a great deal of time before getting back on track. Sadly, almost certain empty-handedness still may not clue *The Secret's* believers into the book's glaring fallacies.

City of the World

We sometimes hear about the concept of time being a necessity on Earth, while in contrast we can see everything happening at once after our soul's consciousness has been activated.

In Earth time, if we were to chronicle life events thus far, we would write in a sequential fashion: "This happened, that happened, then..." So our journal would reflect passages of time and might start with our first memory, followed by milestones from childhood, early adulthood, and so on.

With this in mind, I stumbled upon a movie called *The Music of Chance* (1992), which shows very clearly how we would be able to see all of these events at once. Willy Stone (Joel Grey) creates a maquette (model) he names "City of the World," which fills up a large room and looks like an elaborate train set.

Unlike a train set, this miniature town displays streets, storefronts, clay people, and houses. At the far end of town, we see a replica of Willy's large estate with a long grassy expanse in the back.

Willy explains that this town is where he has always lived. He points to a diminutive street and we see a tiny ceramic couple cuddling a baby in a living room, representing Willy's parents at the time of his birth. We see two figures holding up a piece of paper outside a cigar store, signifying Willy's lottery winnings, which he shared with a friend (Charles Durning).

As the movie unfolds, two workers (Mandy Patinkin and James Spader) build a wall at one end of Willy's estate. With tweezers in hand, Willy updates City of the World every evening. First, he installs a small-scale trailer at the end of the maquette, representing the workers' temporary housing. As the wall construction outside progresses, the replica wall inside expands. Night after night, he adds teeny bricks to the diorama and changes the position of the miniature clay workers near the wall.

City of the World becomes a collection of ersatz snapshots of milestones and lesser events in Willy's life. When viewed from above, we can see all occurrences happening at once. The wall's construction—an ongoing event in one corner—may be *the* event in the characters' lives at that time and it becomes an appendage to the whole miniature town. So, as these characters view City of the World, they see the current construction in relation to Willy's whole life. Past and present may be viewed simultaneously. The changes to the wall are regularly updated to reflect its progress. All other elements are frozen in time, because they represent the past.

Similarly, our soul sees what is happening in a context only comprehensible in another dimension. From the spiritual plane, we may view past, present, and future all at once. We can see everything from a major event, such as childbirth, to a forgettable moment, such as sneezing. This spiritual maquette encompasses movement as well as dozens of locales. City of the World demonstrates how easy this might be.

City of the World shows us that we cannot factor in the future, consider alternative places, or produce motion in a reproduction on this plane. Hence, time and sequential events are necessary for our limited psyches. Consequently, we are shut out from the bigger picture, but certainly would benefit from this fresh and expanded viewpoint, which near-death experiences sometimes offer.

Near-Death Experiences

Reading about near-death experiences (NDEs) reminds us that NDE survivors may have had a brief foray into this perspective. I often thought that an NDE would result in previously inaccessible answers to the big questions. But I soon realized that NDEs have a nasty downside. P.M.H. Atwater tells us that NDE survivors typically return to life accompanied by an alienating aloofness. They expand to love the whole world, but those close at hand often feel neglected, as if the two are mutually exclusive.[55]

Perhaps NDE survivors needed that jolt at the time, but when they revive they face the sometimes long-term medical repercussions of whatever prompted the NDE in the first place. They subsequently "forget" the really important messages, which contain knowledge that would evidently give them an unfair spiritual advantage if remembered.

Apparently, we are all navigating on an even playing field from the spiritual point of view, but our trying times do prompt us to scream foul. Only when faced with prolonged dire circumstances do we truly understand the limits of what we can tolerate. When we are relatively comfortable, the list of situations that we think we could not possibly endure goes on and on. After stumbling through a long, painful trial, the list becomes shorter and sharper.

This brief discussion of enlightenment and consciousness does not fully investigate the depths of these complex topics. Seasoned metaphysical readers will recognize it as merely an introduction, so I leave it to the reader to study further.

Afterword

At the time of this writing, I recognize that I have come a long way, but I still have some distance to cover. I do not have a fully expanded consciousness, nor do I expect to in this lifetime. Nonetheless, I can appreciate great things *as they occur* and enjoy them in hindsight as well. I also consistently identify adversities as opportunities to grow, though it usually takes some time to pinpoint the specific lessons hidden within the hardships.

In the past, while I was surrounded by books and in the midst of Hell, I often asked myself: "When it comes to spiritual matters, what is the truth anyway?"

Metaphysics as Truth

The following represents what I eventually learned about the truth:

First, the truth varies from one individual to another, from one culture to another, and from one religion or philosophy to another. Therefore, the truth is highly subjective and multiple truths often coexist in harmony. Moreover, a collection of compatible truths can be packaged as the foundation of a religion or philosophy.

Second, to qualify as a truth, a given theory must stand the test of time.

Third, when we read metaphysical books, we must distinguish among the responses invoked within us. Some books offer the written version of sedatives. Our need for reassurance and comfort makes us respond favorably to these titles. These books help us feel lulled and soothed.

However, throughout the ages, many authors have addressed the discomforts and mysteries of life. Some of these works have withstood the test of time, while others have drifted into oblivion.

Newer authors research the older works and their manuscripts carry forward certain traditions and leave others behind. These writings also introduce fresh material that reflects the authors' own cultures as well as their individual and collective consciousnesses. Any given theory can morph many times in subsequent generations. Thus, a less reliable signpost of a qualifying truth is the number of writers who have endorsed a specific tradition or philosophy.

The Law of Attraction as Truth

At this juncture, I must acknowledge the countless authors who have promoted the law of attraction since its inception in the late 1800s. Yes, they, too, have carried forward a tradition that seems to be the truth. However, they pander to our egos and our need for wish fulfillment, rather than attempting to disclose the fine points of spirituality. These books simply masquerade as spirituality and digging deeper exposes a large, hollow core.

Intuition, Hunches, and Gut Feelings

Now that we have examined the truth from the writer's perspective, let's look at the reader's point of view. No matter where we live on the planet, what our education level is, or what kind of life we lead, we welcome certain philosophies and reject others.

Accepting specific theories means that we find them intuitively accurate. So, our intuition is the key to all of this because it bridges the gap between our spirit and mind. When our intuition endorses a given theory, then this subjective truth has been tested by our soul. In addition, we may also evaluate a given theory in terms of our own observations and life experiences. These checks and balances help us gain a deeper understanding of spirituality and may even motivate us to take action in a long-neglected area.

Our Soul, Spirit, Intuition, and Mind

"Soul" and "spirit" are often used interchangeably, but subtleties distinguish one from the other. Our souls are everlasting, while our spirits only reflect our Divine nature on Earth.

Whenever I read about the afterlife, I get the distinct impression that our spirit survives death while we are in the first afterlife realm. However, the spirit eventually fuses with the soul after we have climbed up a few astral rungs.

We have already discussed Akashic Records, which chronicle our soul's history, among other things. Our spirit captures a segment of the soul for the purpose of living on Earth. Therefore, the Akashic Records also log the spirit's activity in a given incarnation.

The Relay System

We can discern a distinct pecking order regarding our capacity for cosmic knowledge. At the highest end, our soul is the most expansive element, while the spirit reflects just a fraction of the soul's wisdom. The soul becomes the spirit's mentor, communicating pertinent information at significant times. The spirit then conveys messages to the intuition, which acts like a messenger. When we hear our intuition, our mind responds accordingly. At any point in this relay system, each component translates for the next one down. Let's look at this in another way:

While we are here, our souls communicate with the spirit, but not directly to the mind, as if a chain of command is in place. In turn, our spirit conveys messages to our intuition. We sometimes recognize our intuition through a feeling, which is not easily described. Other times, we hear the "still, small voice" in our heads.

Some people are blessed with very reliable intuitions, while others view intuition as a hit-and-miss proposition. These differences reflect our relative abilities to focus and to keep our minds tranquil for long enough to hear these messages. Practitioners of yoga and meditation tend to have more reliable intuition than do other people.

Generally speaking, women often fare better with their trustworthy intuition than men do. This may result from some men's preference for activity over reflection. However, we all hear some critical communiqués more clearly than others, as if they are much louder. Consequently, people with noisy, hectic lives sometimes heed crucial messages just in the nick of time.

Astronomy, Cosmology, and Metaphysics

An introductory understanding of astronomy makes me see the black holes dotting our galaxy as the most suitable metaphor for metaphysical study. Black holes cannot be directly identified due to their dense nature. Instead, scientists pinpoint a black hole's location by the debris surrounding it. Hence, an astronomer's confidence about a black hole's existence points to an inferential understanding. And so it goes with metaphysicians.

According to cosmic theory, the universe is always expanding. So are our consciousnesses, both individually and collectively. This concept—along with many others discussed herein—refers to invisible phenomena that have so far not been confirmed by empirical evidence. This is not surprising, since the word "metaphysical" can be broken down to mean *beyond (meta) the physical.* This discussion may lead us to ask: "How is it possible to trust what we read?"

Fake versus Authentic Spirituality

As we know by now, I have lots of experience reading about both the law of attraction and spiritual matters that move beyond issues discussed in *The Secret.* I feel that the law of attraction is *faux* spirituality, while many other theories ring true.

I can make this distinction because the failures I experienced by practicing the law of attraction were great enough to remove some of the debris that covered my spirit. By clearing a small path, my soul could more effectively communicate to my spirit and guide me in a more dependable fashion.

Eventually, I could reliably evaluate new ideas as either nonsense, somewhat true, or completely valid, according to the truth I needed to find at that moment. Sometimes our spirits convey messages through hunches. My gut was then able to interpret the value of these writings as I went along, and so it goes with all readers.

Disagreement and Contemplation

Oddly enough, I do not want readers to agree with all of my hypotheses. I prefer to see this book as a potential catalyst for thought. Readers would benefit much more from mulling over a given concept than from accepting it at face value. Hence, rejection of certain passages would actually be the healthiest outcome, due to the highly subjective nature of metaphysics.

Given humanity's ever-evolving intelligence and consciousness, I think we are well equipped today to separate the wheat from the chaff in contemporary metaphysics. Most of us can easily distinguish the self-serving from the sincere and fresh angles from regurgitations. Therefore, the best spiritual books speak to a reader's spirit and appeal to her intellect as well. However, even in such books, the reader still may encounter troublesome or unconvincing passages. Therefore, contemplation is far more important than trusting the written word without question.

Theories that withstand the test of time come from many authors spanning multiple generations and sharing comparable gut reactions. Their instincts corroborate that this material is the truth for them. Since intuition is simply a means of communication from the spirit to the mind, these authors' spirits register the material's soundness before they filter it through their psyches and incorporate influences from their own eras and cultures. By the time they have appended their own unique insights, the resulting passages can sometimes be quite powerful.

As mentioned earlier, spiritual writings may never be scientifically endorsed. Nonetheless, the scientific community accepts many proven phenomena that serve as useful analogies and indirectly confirm spiritual theories. Consider a very old discovery: Dogs have substantially keener senses of hearing and smell than humans do. Hence, this one scientifically verifiable fact illustrates that realities invisible to us coexist with tangible ones. In other words, we can spot the dog, but we cannot *see* his senses. Yet we know they exist.

Hidden Toxins

On that note, I am reminded of David Ewing Duncan's October 2006 article in *National Geographic*, called "The Pollution Within."[56]

National Geographic paid for Duncan to have 320 blood tests and the results included demonstrable levels of:

- A flame-retardant called polybrominated diphenyl ethers (PBDEs). One PBDE in Duncan's system registered 10 times higher than a small study of Americans had revealed, and it was 200 times higher than the amounts found in the average Swede. Doctor Åke Bergman of Stockholm University told Duncan that his frequent flying probably accounted for such levels because aircraft use heavy amounts of flame-retardants
- Leftover toxins from substances that were banned at least a decade ago, such as DDT, lead, PCBs, and dioxins
- Mercury, which rose "from 5 micrograms per liter to a higher-than-recommended 12" after the author consumed freshly caught fish. (Duncan ate halibut one night, followed by swordfish the next morning.) [57]

The author goes on to state that the blood tests revealed many alarming elements that can be traced back to commonly used items, such as cell phones, cleaning products, and shampoos. At the same time, Duncan has a clean bill of health and quotes toxicologist Karl Rozman, who said, "In toxicology, dose is everything."[58]

This research tells me that our bodies host a frightening amount of toxins every day and we simply do not know it because few (if any) symptoms alert us. Duncan's photo suggests he is a robust 40-something, yet his body warehouses untold amounts of pollutants. I say "untold" because the author stopped short of running dozens of other tests that would surely have painted an even bleaker picture.[59]

As we just saw, appearances can be very deceiving and what lies beneath the surface tells us much more than the information available to the naked eye. It boils down to discovering what is already there. The brilliance of this article is due less to Duncan's obvious talent in fleshing out the details and more to his simply conceiving the idea.

This whole exercise serves as a striking metaphor for what is inside us spiritually and what awaits us when the unused portion of our mind becomes activated. We owe it to ourselves to question the state of our spiritual health, as follows:

- Do we hold onto the pollutants shoveled into us from time to time, or do we make a concerted effort to purge them as we go along?
- Have we cleared out enough waste, so our soul can communicate with our spirit?
- Do we spend enough time engaged in spiritually inspired activities as a preventive measure?
- Do we allow time for healing exercises, such as meditation?
- How contaminating are our words and actions to others?

The Last Word about the Law of Attraction

Over the years, law-of-attraction fads have come and gone. No doubt, we will see books like *The Secret* besiege future generations as well. We simply do not like what life dishes out and we want an easy remedy. We will gladly pay for it if we have to.

As our lives go by, one day after another, it may eventually dawn on us that we are not here for the sexy car, the impressive career, or the beautiful home. Once we understand that we have our spiritual work cut out for us, we will make significant spiritual strides. We cannot convert this progress into cash, but we can luxuriate in improved relationships and the satisfaction of knowing that routinely helping others is more rewarding than we ever could have dreamt.

Contact the Author

Share your thoughts about *Burying the Secret* by emailing Carol Rutter at NewAgeJunkie1 at yahoo.com.

Appendix

I have designed the following exercise as an adjunct to Chapter 6. You will need index cards, labeled according to the list below. You can find samples of completed entries at the end of this chapter.

The Elements

People

The key people in your life need a card, whether you love them, dislike them, or have mixed feelings about them.

In some cases, two cards are needed for one name, particularly when the relationship is complicated. For example, we love some people unconditionally, yet some of their habits or characteristics drive us crazy. In this case, the person warrants two cards. Here are the people to include:

- Spouse, or significant other
- Children
- Parents
- Siblings
- Friends (and some acquaintances)

- Certain coworkers
- Certain relatives
- Anyone with whom you are now spending a lot of time.

Life Circumstances

Please make one card for each, though some may warrant two cards:

- Finances
- Job
- Career
- Health
- Social Life
- Home Life Atmosphere
- Sex Life
- Creativity
- Alone Time
- Groups/Associations
- Place of Worship
- Escapist Activities.

Before you categorize these into *Mostly Pleasure, Mostly Pain,* or *Non-applicable*, you must evaluate their current status in your psyche. For any category that seems *Non-applicable*, you must figure out if you still have any emotional baggage associated with them. For example, my mother died 20 years ago, but I am still dealing with her legacy today, whereas I have no children and I am totally at peace with that. So I would have to categorize my mother as still *Mostly Painful* and children as *Non-applicable*. Someone who had no children and desperately wanted them would categorize them as *Mostly Painful.*

Similarly, one person with no job may be financially set enough to feel free and happy, while another may be greatly troubled by unemployment. Therefore, any emotional reaction precludes using the *Non-applicable* category.

Relationships

First, let's look at relationships. Think about what has been going on lately with each one. If you feel that a given individual represents part pain and part pleasure, then make up a second card with that person's name on it. List the causes of pain on one card and the sources of pleasure on the other. Avoid citing minor annoyances and stick to important issues.

Finances

In this area, your net worth is less of an issue than how much time you spend fretting about money or reaping its rewards.

Job

If you do not have a job, are you OK with that? If you are employed, how is the work itself? The company's treatment of you? Your superiors? Coworkers? If a coworker is either an ally or a foe, make a card for that person, too.

Career

Are you in the career of your dreams? If not, are you taking steps to correct that? How do you feel about your current career status?

Health

If you do not think much about your health, it belongs in the *Mostly Pleasure* category. However, if you are currently undergoing medical treatments, how optimistic do you feel about a full recovery? Are you plagued by a chronic, incurable condition? Make a card for that ailment. What about insomnia or so-called "lifestyle" issues, such as obesity and smoking? Make cards for these as well.

Social Life

How is your social life? Are you geographically isolated from your desired social life? What components would constitute a desirable social life? How close are you to that now?

Home Life Atmosphere

When you open the door to your home, what kind of atmosphere greets you? Is this a place of love and comfort, or can you cut the tension with a knife? Is your home reasonably tidy, or so messy that you can never find anything?

Sex Life

How is your sex life? If you have a partner, how satisfied are you? If you do not currently have a partner, is your absent sex life a source of distress?

Creativity

Do you have time to develop your creativity? If so, are you satisfied with the time you spend on this activity? If not, how deprived do you feel?

Alone Time

Do you get enough alone time or too much? How do you feel when you are alone?

Groups/Associations

Do these groups represent harmony and pleasure or conflict and tension? How do you evaluate your role: Are you comfortable or do you feel used? Are you getting what you anticipated when you first joined?

Place of Worship

Is your psyche completely in sync with the teachings of this place of worship? Do you feel that you are growing as a result of your participation, or do you feel spiritually stagnant?

Escapist Activities

Escapist activities include pastimes, such as playing a musical instrument, bowling, knitting, etc. Are they truly sources of pleasure, or candidates for addiction?

Interpreting the Results

Now you have a bunch of cards divided into three categories. Set aside the *Non-applicable* for a moment and rearrange the other two categories in descending order of importance. For example, put the source of greatest happiness at the beginning of *Mostly Pleasure* and the most irksome one at the top of *Mostly Pain*. Arrange them in columns, so you can see them all at the same time.

The *Mostly Pleasure* list shows all your support systems. The *Mostly Pain* list highlights all your current arenas for lessons, or areas ripe for change. One by one, study each *Mostly Pain* card and apply the questions addressed in the last segment. To better understand an agitating element, you must ask: Does this person or situation:

- Reflect some characteristic of yours?
- Invoke a significant response? Upon deeper analysis, what does this mirror in you?
- Provide nonstop stress as inducement for change? If so, what change?
- Unknowingly supply an analogy, or a common link between you and the person or situation?
- Introduce a fresh viewpoint? This would apply to a person or situation that is very different from what you are used to, something that introduces you to a novel way of thinking. In some instances, this could mean an opportunity to re-examine your belief system. These people or situations may end up in the *Mostly Pain* pile because they shake your foundation on some level.

Try to establish similarities among the *Mostly Pain* cards. Do you see any recurring motifs? Is it possible that the same lesson takes different forms? Can you identify people who irritate you in the same way as figures from the past have done?

The *Mostly Pleasure* cards are important, too. As you experience adversity, you want to cushion yourself with as much support as possible while you try to decipher the lessons hidden in the painful situations. So, you might want to draw more from these people and situations during a rough period, whether it involves confiding in a friend or seeing a double feature at the cinema. The worst thing would be to allow self-pity to wash over you for extended periods. The best strategy entails working through the problem with an understanding ally.

The *Non-applicable* cards can usually be discarded, though they should be studied first. In the fictional array of cards below, you will see "deceased father" and "groups/associations" under *Non-applicable*. Let's assume that the creator of this list is at peace with her father's memory, but in the future she may want to join a career group to broaden her professional contacts. Therefore, certain *Non-applicable* items might be future candidates for the *Mostly Pleasure* list.

Shuffle Them Up

You might also want to re-do this exercise in two different ways:

First, reconfigure the cards to reflect your situation five years ago. This should emphasize the areas of improvement and decline and remind you of spiritual milestones.

Second, rearrange the cards to show your aspirations for five years from now. If you reallocate all the *Mostly Pain* cards into either *Non-applicable* or *Mostly Pleasure*, you have to figure out what steps you must take to accomplish this.

The most valuable part of this exercise pertains to its potential for uprooting unconscious elements and bringing them into conscious awareness. Also, if you keep returning to the *Mostly Pain* cards and try to decipher the implied lessons, you might just crack the case over time.

You should be motivated to do so, because once the lesson is integrated, the difficult person and/or situation fades away or your perception becomes so radically altered that they cease to bother you.

You also might want to enlist a friend to help you figure all this out, because fresh insights, offered at the right time, can dramatically catapult conscious comprehension of a previously mysterious and confusing situation. Or, you could do the exercise by yourself first and then a second time with an ally.

Check out a fictional array of cards:

Mostly Pleasure

Husband Damon (first card)

Incredibly supportive of everything I do
Wonderful with the kids
Dotes on me when I'm sick

Son Miles

Sunny disposition, easy-going, and funny
Helps out a lot
Impressive grades at school
Reliable and responsible beyond his years

Friend Susan

A great listener
Entertaining raconteur
Offers constructive suggestions
I always feel much better after talking to her

Mother (first card)

Educated, witty, and a great conversationalist
Well-connected and willing to hook me up

Coworker Becky

Always fun and a fantastic lunch companion

Keeps me in the loop about office matters, including corporate affairs and gossip

Willing to baby-sit with little notice

Job (first card)

Pays well

State-of-the-art technology

Lots of attractive perks

Four weeks vacation

Social Life

Great—there is always something going on

Place of Worship

Fantastic Rabbi

Warm, supportive atmosphere

Mostly Pain

Daughter Ashley

My greatest source of worry and stress

In with the wrong crowd

Shows signs of regular drug use

Takes the car without asking

Constantly displays sullenness and defiance

Lies all the time

Never listens

Coworker Brandon

Passive-aggressive to the max

Takes advantage of every opportunity to sabotage me
After my daughter Ashley, he pushes my buttons the most

Husband Damon (second card)

Will not do a lick of work around the house
Refuses to go to the doctor for regular diabetes treatment
Irresponsible about spending
Snores loudly enough that I often sleep on the couch
Withdraws when he feels confronted
Addicted to sports on TV
Allows friends to drop by without calling first

Mother (second card)

Chronic alcoholic
Calls at all hours in a drunken stupor
Tries to micromanage my life
Conveys a sense of conditional love and approval
Rarely acknowledges that I am not her clone

Finances

A complete mess

Job (second card)

No sense of accomplishment
Tedious and repetitive
Corporate instability looming
Feeling trapped

Smoking

Still smoking 10 a day
Coughing more than I used to

Weight

Still two sizes bigger than most of my wardrobe

Crohn's Disease

Still painful and occasionally embarrassing.

Career

Not a chance in the foreseeable future of ever working at a job that reflects my passion and education

Sex Life

When Damon and I make love every other month, we are doing quite well. Usually, it is three or four times a year. I miss the passion we used to enjoy.

Alone Time

What's that?

Non-applicable

My deceased father
Groups/Associations

Notes

Chapter 1. Confessions of a New Age Junkie

1. Golas, *The Lazy Man's Guide to Enlightenment*, 6.

Chapter 2. Snake Oil, P.T. Barnum, and *The Secret*

2. Ressner, "The Secret of Success."
3. Byrne, *The Secret,* xiii-xiv.
4. Ressner, "The Secret of Success," and *PR Newswire*, "Carolyn K. Reidy Named President and Chief Executive Officer of Simon & Schuster, Inc."
5. Ray's website.
6. Ressner, "The Secret of Success."
7. Byrne, *The Secret,* Copyright page.
8. The Project for Excellence in Journalism, "Ownership."
9. Rapaille, *The Culture Code,* 17.
10. Ibid.
11. Holland, "The Tyranny of Positive Thinking."
12. Ibid.
13. Ibid.
14. Myer, *The New Medicine.*
15. Byrne, *The Secret,* Copyright page.
16. Wise County Messenger, "Tinkham Believes She Can Cure her Breast Cancer Herself."
17. PR Newswire, "Carolyn K. Reidy Named President and Chief Executive Officer of Simon & Schuster, Inc."
18. Ressner, "The Secret of Success."
19. Adler, "Decoding the Secret."

Chapter 3. The Laws Governing External Sources of Suffering

20. Goldsmith, *Living the Infinite Way*, 100.
21. Gonzalez-Balado, *My Life for the Poor*, 104.

Chapter 4. The Laws Governing Internal Sources of Suffering

22. Bly, *A Little Book on the Human Shadow*, 4.
23. Miller, *The Drama of the Gifted Child*, 101-113.
24. Harrison, *Love Your Disease*, 18.
25. Miller, *The Drama of the Gifted Child*, 101-113.
26. Abrams, *Reclaiming the Inner Child*, 198-203.
27. Jung, *The Portable Jung*, 13.
28. Wikipedia on chemical imbalances.
29. Myss, *Why People Don't Heal / Three Levels of Power.*
30. Ibid.
31. Ibid.

Chapter 5. The Laws of Transition—The Prebirth Agenda

32. Bache, *Lifecycles: Reincarnation and the Web of Life*, 19.
33. Taylor, "The Religious and Other Beliefs of Americans 2003." and Harris Interactive (no author cited) "The Religious and Other Beliefs of Americans 2005." Separate Harris polls, indicate 21 percent (December 2005) and 27 percent (February 2003) respectively. Other websites quote several different points in between 21 percent and 27 percent.
34. ReligiousTolerance.org cites the following poll within Religious Beliefs of Americans (no author cited): Survey Research Center at the University of California at Berkeley CA, reported in the Globe and Mail (Toronto, ON) newspaper on Oct 9, 1999.
35. Klimo and Heath, Suicide: *What Really Happens in the Afterlife?* 108.

36. Ibid.

Chapter 6. The Laws of Transition—Our Sacred Purpose

37. Wolfe, *Lackawanna Blues.*
38. Vranich, *Anderson Cooper 360.*
39. Pinsky, *Anderson Cooper 360.*
40. Schickel, *Spielberg on Spielberg.*
41. Schilling, *God and Human Anguish*, 66.
42. Underhill, *The Spiritual Life*, 85, 89.

Chapter 7. The Law of Cause and Effect—Karma

43. Chapotin, "Karma Re-examined," 170.
44. Ibid.
45. Klimo and Heath, *Suicide: What Really Happens in the Afterlife?* 114.
46. Ibid.

Chapter 8. The Law We Consciously Control—Free Will

47. World Press (no author cited), "Osama Bin Laden: CIA's Toy Gone Awry."
48. Ibid.

Chapter 9. Religion, Spirituality, and Prayers

49. Game Plan greeting card, serial number B-259275.
50. Age of the Sage, *Jiddu Krishnamurti Biography.*
51. Krishnamurti, *Lecture Given by J. Krishnamurti . . . .*
52. Ibid.
53. Golas. *The Lazy Man's Guide to Enlightenment*, 32.

Chapter 10. Enlightenment and Consciousness

54. Combs and Holland, *Synchronicity: Science, Myth and the Trickster,* 17.
55. Atwater, *Coming Back to Life,* 14.

Conclusion

56. Duncan, "The Pollution Within."
57. Ibid.
58. Ibid.
59. Duncan, "The Pollution Within" and Duncan's website.

Works Cited

A

Abrams, Jeremiah, ed. 1990. *Reclaiming the Inner Child*. Los Angeles: Tarcher.

Adler, Jerry. March 5, 2007. "Decoding the Secret," *Newsweek*. http://www.msnbc.msn.com/id/17314883/site/newsweek/

Age of the Sage (no author or date cited). "Jiddu Krishnamurti Biography." http://www.age-of-the-sage.org/theosophy/krishnamurti.html

Atwater, P.M.H. 1988. *Coming Back to Life: The After Effects of The Near Death Experience*. New York: Dodd Mead.

B

Bache, Christopher M. 1990. *Lifecycles: Reincarnation and the Web of Life*. New York: Paragon.

Bhushan, Ranjit. Sept. 17, 2001. "Osama Bin Laden: CIA's Toy Gone Awry." *Outlook*. In *World Press Review*, Vol. 48, #11. http://www.worldpress.org/1101binladen_cia.htm

Bly, Robert. 1988. *A Little Book on the Human Shadow*. San Francisco: Harper.

Byrne, Rhonda, ed. 2006. *The Secret*. New York: Atria Books / Beyond Words.

C

Carter, Thomas, Fred Gerber and Bobby Roth, directors. 2002-2004. *Hack*. Television. Production companies: Big Ticket Productions and CBS Television.

Chapotin, Diana Cunningham. 1990. "Karma Re-examined." In *Karma: Rhythmic Return to Harmony*, edited by V. Hansen, 170. Wheaton IL: Quest Books..

Combs, Allan and Mark Holland. 1990. *Synchronicity: Science, Myth and the Trickster*. New York: Paragon.

D

DeNiro, Robert, director. 1993. *A Bronx Tale*. Feature film. Production companies: B.T. Films, Penta Entertainment, Price Entertainment, and Tribeca Productions.

Dictionary.com. http://www.dictionary.com

Duncan, David Ewing. October 2006. "The Pollution Within," *National Geographic*. http://www3.nationalgeographic.com/ngm/0610/feature4/index.html and http://www.davidewingduncan.net/about_david.htm

E & F

Einstein, Albert (no date cited). In *The Secret* DVD, directed by Drew Heriot. Production companies: Prime Time Productions, Nine Network Australia, and T.S. Production.

Forbes Magazine (no author or date cited). "Forbes 100 List." *Forbes*. http://www.forbes.com/lists/2007/53/07celebrities_Rhonda-Byrne_JYV0.html

G

Game Plan greeting card, serial number B-259275. Date and place unknown.

Golas, Thaddeus. 1971. *The Lazy Man's Guide to Enlightenment*. Palo Alto, CA: Seed Center.

Goldsmith, Joel S. 1961. *Living the Infinite Way*. New York: Harper.

Gonzalez-Balado, Jose Luis, and Janet N. Playfoot, eds. 1985. *My Life for the Poor: Mother Teresa of Calcutta*. San Francisco: Harper.

H

Haas, Philip, director. 1993. *The Music of Chance*. Feature film. Production companies: I.R.S. and Transatlantic Release.

Harris Interactive, (no author cited). 2006. *The Religious and Other Beliefs of Americans 2005*. http://www.harrisinteractive.com/harris_poll/index.

asp?PID=618. See also: Taylor, Humphrey. 2004. *The Religious and Other Beliefs of Americans 2003.* http://www.harrisinteractive.com/harris_poll/index.asp?PID=359

Harrison, John W. 1984. *Love Your Disease.* Santa Monica, CA: Hay House.

Hay, Louise L. 1984. *You Can Heal Your Life.* Santa Monica, CA: Hay House.

———. 1982. *Heal Your Body.* Santa Monica, CA: Hay House.

Heriot, Drew. 2006. *The Secret.* DVD. Production companies: Prime Time Productions, Nine Network Australia, and T.S. Production.

Holland, Jimmie. 2001. "The Tyranny of Positive Thinking," adapted from the book, *The Human Side of Cancer, Living with Hope, Coping with Uncertainty,* by Jimmie Holland and Sheldon Lewis. New York: Harper, 2001. See also http://www.humansideofcancer.com/chapter2/chapter.2.htm and http://www.leukemia-lymphoma.org/all_page?item_id=7038

J

Jung, Carl G. 1971. *The Portable Jung.* New York: Viking.

———. 1954. "The Development of Personality," *CW,* Vol. 17, paragraph 84.

K

Kelley, David E., creator. 1994-2000. *Chicago Hope.* Television. Production companies: 20th Century Fox Television and David E. Kelley Productions.

Klane, Robert, director. 1993. *Weekend at Bernie's.* Feature film. Production companies: Artimm, D&A Partnership, TriStar Pictures, and Victor Drai Productions.

Klimo, John and Pamela Rae Heath. 2006. *Suicide: What Really Happens in the Afterlife?* Berkeley, CA: North Atlantic Books.

Koestler, Arthur. 1972. *The Roots of Coincidence.* New York: Vintage.

Krishnamurti, Jiddu, about. (No author or date cited.) "Jiddu Krishnamurti

Biography." http://www.age-of-the-sage.org/theosophy/krishnamurti.html

Krishnamurti, Jiddu. 1929. "Lecture Given by J. Krishnamurti, in 1929, When He Dissolved the Order of the Star of the East." http://www.katinkahesselink.net/kr/star.htm

M

Miller, Alice. 1981. *The Drama of the Gifted Child* (formerly *Prisoners of Childhood*). New York: Basic.

Montana, Tony and Mark Brian Smith, directors. 2003. *Overnight*. Documentary. Production companies: Think Film and Black & White Pictures.

Myer, Muffie, director. 2006. *The New Medicine*. Documentary. Production companies: Gorton Studios and Twin Cities Public Television.

Myss, Caroline. 2004. *Why People Don't Heal / Three Levels of Power*. DVD. Production company: Wellspring.

P

Peale, Norman Vincent. 1978. *The Power of Positive Thinking*. Pawling NY: Peale Center for Christian Living.

Pinsky, Drew. August 27, 2007. CNN. *Anderson Cooper 360*.

Price, William Randolph. 1975. *The Superbeings* New York: Ballantine.

PR Newswire (no author cited). September 6, 2007. "Carolyn K. Reidy Named President and Chief Executive Officer of Simon & Schuster, Inc.," CNNMoney.com. http://money.cnn.com/news/newsfeeds/articles/prnewswire/YTH03006092007-1.htm

Project for Excellence in Journalism, The. 2006. "Ownership." *The State of the News Media*. http://www.stateofthenewsmedia.org/2006/narrative_networktv_ownership.asp?cat=5&media=5

R

Rapaille, Clotaire. 2007. *The Culture Code*. New York: Broadway.

Ray, James. (no date cited). List of speaking engagements. http://jamesray.

com/events/creating-wealth-experience.php

Reeve, Christopher. 1999. *Still Me.* New York: Ballantine.

Religious Tolerance (no author or date cited). *Religious Beliefs of Americans.* http://www.religioustolerance.org/chr_poll3.htm

Ressner, Jeffrey. December 26, 2006. "The Secret of Success," *Time.*

S

Schickel, Richard, director. 2007. *Spielberg on Spielberg.* Documentary. Production company: TMC.

Scorsese, Martin, director. 1990. *Goodfellas.* Feature Film. Production company: Warner Bros.

Shilling, Paul. 1977. *God and Human Anguish.* Nashville, TN: Abingdon.

Short, Susanne. 1990. "Whispering of the Walls." In *Reclaiming the Inner Child,* edited by Jeremiah Abrams. Los Angeles: Tarcher.

Styron, William. 1990. *Darkness Visible.* New York: Random House.

T

Taylor, Humphrey. 2004. *The Religious and Other Beliefs of Americans 2003.*

http://www.harrisinteractive.com/harris_poll/index.asp?PID=359. See also Harris Interactive. 2006. (no author cited). *The Religious and Other Beliefs of Americans 2005.* http://www.harrisinteractive.com/harris_poll/index.asp?PID=618

Thomson, Sandra. A. 1994. *Cloud Nine: A Dreamer's Dictionary.* New York: Avon.

Todeschi, Kevin J. 1998. *Edgar Cayce on the Akashic Records.* Virginia Beach, VA: A.R.E. Press. http://www.edgarcayce.org/about_ec/cayce_on/akashic/

U & V

Underhill, Evelyn. 1936. *The Spiritual Life.* New York: Harper. See also http://www.mrrena.com/misc/sl.shtml

Vranich, Belisa. August 27, 2007. CNN. *Anderson Cooper 360.*

W

Wikipedia. No author or date cited. "Chemical Imbalances in Clinical Depression." http://en.wikipedia.org/wiki/Chemical_imbalance_theory#Clinical_depression

———. No author or date cited. "Alternative Medicine." http://en.wikipedia.org/wiki/Alternative_medicine

———. No author or date cited. "Carl Jung." http://en.wikipedia.org/wiki/Carl_Jung

———. No author or date cited. "Alice Miller." http://en.wikipedia.org/wiki/Alice_Miller_%28psychologist%29

Wise County Messenger (no author cited). April 1, 2007. "Kim Tinkham Believes She Can Cure her Breast Cancer Herself." http://www.wcmessenger.com/news/news/EEZVuVFyFZvtdbUrLt.php

Wolfe, George C., director. 2005. *Lackawanna Blues.* Feature film. Production companies: HBO Films and HBO Pictures.

Bibliography

This multimedia reference list contains several sections. Some entries repeat after the A-Z list under Articles, DVD Lectures, Films, and Online References. In addition, articles found online usually appear three times: In Articles, Online References, and the A-Z list. Some entries in the TV Shows section are not in the A-Z list.

A

Abrams, Jeremiah, ed. *Reclaiming the Inner Child*. Los Angeles: Tarcher, 1990.

Adler, Jerry. "Decoding the Secret," *Newsweek*, March 5, 2007. http://www.msnbc.msn.com/id/17314883/site/newsweek/

Age of the Sage (no author cited). "Jiddu Krishnamurti Biography." http://www.age-of-the-sage.org/theosophy/krishnamurti.html

Allen, James. *From Poverty to Power*. Santa Fe, NM: Sun Books, 1989.

Anderson, Walt. *Open Secrets: A Western Guide to Tibetan Buddhism*. New York: Penguin, 1979.

Arkin, Alan. *Halfway Through the Door*. New York: Harper, 1979.

Armstrong, Karen. *Visions of God*. New York: Bantam, 1994.

Arts, Herwig. *God, The Christian and Human Suffering*. Collegeville, MN: The Liturgical Press, 1993.

Atwater, P.M.H. *Coming Back to Life: The After Effects of The Near Death Experience*. New York: Dodd Mead, 1988.

B

Babbie, Earl. *You Can Make a Difference*. New York: St. Martin's, 1985.

Bach, Marcus. *The Challenge of Change*. Lee's Summit, MO: Unity, 1967.

Bache, Christopher M. *Lifecycles: Reincarnation and the Web of Life*. New

York: Paragon, 1990.
Baha'u'llah. *The Seven Valleys and the Four Valleys.* Wilmette, IL: Baha'i Publishing Trust, 1945.
Barett, William. *Death of the Soul.* New York: Doubleday, 1986.
Bateson, Gregory. *Steps to an Ecology of Mind.* New York: Ballantine, 1972.
Beck, Sanderson and Mark T. Holmes, eds. *Across the Golden Bridge.* Los Angeles: Golden Age Education, 1974.
Beveridge, W. I. B. *Seeds of Discovery.* New York: Norton, 1980.
Bhaktivedanta, A.C. (Swami Prabhupada). *Bhagavad-Gita As It Is.* Los Angeles: Bhaktivedanta Book Trust, 1968.
Bhushan, Ranjit. "Osama Bin Laden: CIA's Toy Gone Awry." *Outlook.* In *World Press Review,* Vol. 48, #11, September 17, 2001. http://www.worldpress.org/1101binladen_cia.htm
Bly, Robert. *A Little Book on the Human Shadow.* San Francisco: Harper, 1988.
Bolen, Jean S. *The Tao of Psychology.* New York: Harper, 1979.
Bosnak, Robert. *A Little Course in Dreams.* Boston: Shambhala, 1988.
Bradford, Amory, H. *The Ascent of the Soul.* New York: The Outlook Company, 1902.
Bradshaw, John. *Healing the Shame That Binds You.* Deerfield Beach, FL: Health Communications Inc, 1988.
———. *Homecoming.* New York: Bantam, 1990.
Bragdon, Emma. *The Call of Spiritual Emergency.* San Francisco: Harper, 1990.
Brandon, David. *Zen in the Art of Helping.* New York: Dell, 1976.
Bridges, William. *Transitions: Making Sense of Life's Changes.* Menlo Park, CA: Addison-Welsley, 1980.
Brinkley, Dannion. *Saved By the Light.* New York: Villard, 1994.
Bro, Harman Hartzell. *Begin a New Life: The Approach of Edgar Cayce.* New York: Harper, 1971.
Brown, Beth. *Play Your Hunch-Make it a Miracle!* New York: Hawthorn,

1967.

Bucke, Richard Morris. *Cosmic Consciousness.* Secaucus, NJ: Citadel, 1961.

Byrne, Rhonda, ed. *The Secret.* New York: Atria Books/Beyond Words, 2006.

C

Callanan, Maggie and Patricia Kelley. *Final Gifts: Understand the Special Awareness, Needs and Communication of the Dying.* New York: Poseidon, 1992.

Capps, Walter H, and Wendy M, Wright, eds. *Silent Fire: An Invitation to Western Mysticism.* San Francisco: Harper, 1978.

Capra, Fritjof. *The Turning Point: Science, Society and the Rising Culture.* New York: Simon & Schuster, 1982.

———. *Uncommon Wisdom: Conversations with Remarkable People.* New York: Simon & Schuster, 1988.

Carter, Mary Ellen. *My Years With Edgar Cayce: The Personal Story of Gladys Davis Turner.* New York: Harper, 1972.

Carter, Thomas, Fred Gerber and Bobby Roth, Directors. *Hack.* Television. Production companies: Big Ticket Productions and CBS Television, 2002-2004.

Cather, Willa and Georgine Milmine. *The Life Of Mary Baker Eddy and The History of Christian Science.* Lincoln, NE: University of Nebraska Press, 1993.

Cerminara, Gina. *Many Mansions.* New York: Morrow, 1950.

———. *The World Within.* New York: Morrow, 1957.

Chapotin, Diana Cunningham. "Karma Re-examined." In *Karma: Rhythmic Return to Harmony,* edited by V. Hansen, 170. Wheaton IL: Quest Books, 1990.

Chopra, Deepak. *The Seven Spiritual Laws of Success.* San Rafael, CA: Amber-Allen, 1994.

———. *Unconditional Life: Mastering the Forces That Shape Personal*

Reality. New York: Bantam, 1989.

Christopher, Milbourne. *Search for the Soul*. New York: Thomas Y. Crowell, 1979.

Cochran, Lin. *Edgar Cayce on Secrets of the Universe and How to Use Them in Your Life*. New York: Warner, 1989.

Combs, Allan and Mark Holland. *Synchronicity: Science, Myth and the Trickster*. New York: Paragon, 1990.

Corlett, William and John Moore. *The Buddha Way*. Scarsdale, NY: Bradbury, 1979.

Cronkite, Kathy. *On the Edge of Darkness: Conversations About Conquering Depression*. New York: Doubleday, 1994.

Cousins, Norman. *Dr Schweitzer of Lambarene*. New York: Harper, 1960.

———. *Anatomy of an Illness*. New York: Norton, 1979.

Culligan, Joseph. *When in Doubt Check Him Out*. Miami, FL: Hallmark, 1993.

D

Daniels, Victor & Laurence Horowitz. *Being and Caring*. Palo Alto, CA: Mayfield, 1976.

Dass, Ram. *Journey of Awakening*. New York: Bantam, 1978.

Dass, Ram and Paul Gorman. *How Can I Help?* New York: Knopf, 1985.

Delany, Sarah and A. Elizabeth Delany. *The Delany Sisters' Book of Everyday Wisdom*. New York: Kodansha International, 1994.

Dement, William C. *Some Must Watch While Some Must Sleep*. San Francisco: W.H. Freeman, 1972.

DeNiro, Robert, director. *A Bronx Tale*. Feature film. Production companies: B.T. Films, Penta Entertainment, Price Entertainment, and Tribeca Productions, 1993.

Dobson, James. *When God Doesn't Make Sense*. Wheaton, IL: Tyndale Rouser, 1993.

Dreher, Diane. *The Tao of Peace*. New York: Donald I. Fine, 1990.

Dresser, Annetta Gertrude. *The Philosophy of P.P. Quimby*. New York: The Builders Press, 1895.

Duncan, David Ewing. "The Pollution Within," *National Geographic*, October 2006. http://www3.nationalgeographic.com/ngm/0610/feature4/index.html and http://www.davidewingduncan.net/about_david.htm

Dyer, Wayne W. *Real Magic*. New York: Harper, 1992.

———. *You'll See It When You Believe It*. New York: Morrow, 1989.

E

Eadie, Betty J. *Embraced By the Light*. Placerville, CA: Gold Leaf, 1992.

Eighner, Lars. *Travels With Lizbeth*. New York: St. Martin's, 1993.

Einstein, Albert. In *The Secret*, directed by Drew Heriot. DVD. Production companies: Prime Time Productions, Nine Network Australia, and T.S. Production, no date cited.

Eliade, Mircea. *The Myth of the Eternal Return*. Princeton, NJ: Princeton University Press, 1954.

Elgin, Duane. *Voluntary Simplicity*. New York: Morrow, 1981.

Estes, Clarissa Pinkola. *Women Who Run With the Wolves*. New York: Ballantine, 1992.

Estess, Ted L. *Elie Wiesel*. New York: Frederick Unger, 1980.

Evely, Louis. *Suffering*. New York: Herder & Herder, 1967.

F

Fankhauser, Jerry. *The Power of Affirmations*. Houston, TX: Jerry Fankhauser, 1983.

Ferguson, Marilyn. *The Aquarian Conspiracy*. Los Angeles: Tarcher, 1980.

Feschotte, Jacques. *Albert Schweitzer: An Introduction*. Boston: Beacon, 1955.

Field, Sidney. *Krishnamurti: The Reluctant Messiah*. New York: Paragon, 1989.

Fisher, Mark. *The Instant Millionaire.* San Rafael, CA: New World Library, 1990.

Forbes Magazine (no author cited). "Forbes 100 List," *Forbes.* http://www.forbes.com/lists/2007/53/07celebrities_Rhonda-Byrne_JYV0.html

Fox, Matthew. *On Becoming a Musical Mystical Bear: Spirituality American Style.* New York: Paulist, 1972.

———. *Whee! We, wee. All the Way Home.* Santa Fe, NM: Bear & Co., 1981.

Franck, Frederick. *Days With Albert Schweitzer: A Lambarene Landscape.* New York: Henry Holt, 1959.

Frankl, Viktor Emil. *Man's Search for Meaning.* Boston: Beacon, 1959.

Fremantle, Francesca and Chogyam Trungpa, translated and commentary by. *The Tibetan Book of the Dead.* Boston: Shambhala, 1975.

Fulghum, Robert. *All Really Need to Know I Learned in Kindergarten.* New York: Villard, 1989.

G

Gabrin, Kahlil. *The Prophet.* New York: Knopf, 1923.

Game Plan greeting card, serial number B-259275. Date and place unknown.

Gawain, Shakti. *Living in the Light.* San Rafael, CA: New World Library, 1986.

———. *Creative Visualization.* Mill Valley, CA: Whatever, 1979.

Gendlin, Eugene. *Focusing.* New York: Bantam, 1978.

Gillies, Jerry. *Money-Love.* New York: Warner, 1978.

Golas, Thaddeus. *The Lazy Man's Guide to Enlightenment.* Palo Alto, CA: Seed Center, 1971.

Goldberg, Philip. *The Intuitive Edge: Understanding and Developing Intuition.* Los Angeles: Tarcher, 1983.

Goldsmith, Joel S. *Awakening Mystical Consciousness.* New York: Harper. 1980.

———. *Beyond Words and Thoughts.* Secaucus, NJ: Citadel, 1968.

———. *Leave Your Nets*. Secaucus, NJ: Citadel, 1964.
———. *Living By Grace*. New York: Harper, 1984.
———. *Living the Infinite Way*. New York: Harper, 1961.
———. *The Mystical I*. New York: Harper, 1971.
———. *Our Spiritual Resources*. New York: Harper, 1978.
———. *The Thunder of Silence*. New York: Harper, 1961.
———. *The World is New*. New York: Harper, 1962.
Goldstein, Joseph. *The Experience of Insight*. Boston: Shambhala, 1987.
Gonzalez-Balado, Jose Luis, and Janet N. Playfoot, eds. *My Life for the Poor: Mother Teresa of Calcutta*. San Francisco: Harper, 1985.
Goodman, Michael H. *The Last Dalai Lama*. Boston: Shambhala, 1986.
Gordon, Anne. *A Book of Saints*. New York: Bantam, 1994.
Govinda, Lama. *Insights of a Himalayan Pilgrim*. Berkeley, CA: Dharma, 1991.
Griffin, William. *Clive Staples Lewis: A Dramatic Life*. San Francisco: Harper, 1986.
Grof, Christina and Stanislav Grof. *The Stormy Search for the Self.* Los Angeles: Tarcher, 1990.
Grof, Stanislav and Christine Grof, eds. *Spiritual Emergency: When Personal Transformation Becomes a Crisis*. Los Angeles: Tarcher, 1989.
Gurdjieff, G.I. *Meetings With Remarkable Men*. New York: Dutton, 1969.
Gyatso, Tenzin, His Holiness The Dalai Lama of Tibet. *The Dalai Lama at Harvard*. Ithaca, NY: Snow Lions, 1988.

H

Haas, Philip, director. *The Music of Chance*. Feature film. Production companies: I.R.S. and Transatlantic Release, 1993.
Hall, James A. *The Jungian Experience: Analysis and Individuation*. Toronto: Inner City, 1986.
Hall, Manly P. *Death and After*. Los Angeles: The Philosophical Research Society, 1929.

———. *Death to Rebirth.* Los Angeles: The Philosophical Research Society, 1979.

———. *Twelve World Teachers.* Los Angeles: The Philosophical Research Society, 1965.

Hanh, Thich Nhat. *The Miracle of Mindfulness.* Boston: Beacon, 1975.

Hansen, V., ed. *Karma: Rhythmic Return to Harmony.* Wheaton, IL: Quest, 1990.

Harkness, Georgia. *The Dark Night of the Soul.* New York: Abingdon-Cokesbury, 1945.

Harner, Michael. *The Way of the Shaman.* New York: Bantam, 1980.

Harris Interactive (no author cited). *The Religious and Other Beliefs of Americans 2005*, 2006. http://www.harrisinteractive.com/harris_poll/index.asp?PID=618. See also: Taylor, Humphrey. *The Religious and Other Beliefs of Americans 2003*, 2004. http://www.harrisinteractive.com/harris_poll/index.asp?PID=359.

Harrison, John W. *Love Your Disease.* Santa Monica, CA: Hay House, 1984.

Hay, Louise L. *You Can Heal Your Life.* Santa Monica, CA: Hay House, 1984.

———. *Heal Your Body.* Santa Monica, CA: Hay House, 1982.

Hazzard, Tony. *Dreams and Their Meanings.* London: Ward Lock, 1989.

Henderson, Joseph L. *Shadow and Self.* Wilmette, IL: Chiron, 1990.

Heriot, Drew. *The Secret.* DVD. Production companies: Prime Time Productions, Nine Network Australia, and T.S. Production, 2006.

Hofstadter, Douglas and Daniel C. Dennett, eds. *The Mind's I: Fantasies and Reflections on Self and Soul.* New York: Basic, 1981.

Holland, Jimmie. "The Tyranny of Positive Thinking," adapted from the book, *The Human Side of Cancer, Living with Hope, Coping with Uncertainty*, by Jimmie Holland and Sheldon Lewis. New York: Harper, 2001. See also http://www.humansideofcancer.com/chapter2/chapter.2.htm and http://www.leukemia-lymphoma.org/all_page?item_id=7038

Holmes, Fenwicke L. *Ernest Holmes: His Life and Times.* New York: Dodd Mead, 1970.

Hooper, Walter. *Through Joy and Beyond.* New York: MacMillan, 1982.

Hotchkiss, Burt. *Have Miracles, Will Travel.* Detroit: Harlo, 1982.

Howard, Vernon. *Esoteric Mind-Power.* Lakemont, GA: CSA, 1973.

———. *The Mystic Path to Cosmic Power.* West Nyack, NY: Parker, 1967.

———. *Pathways to Perfect Living.* New York: Stein and Day, 1969.

———. *The Power of Your Supermind.* Marina del Rey, CA: DeVorss, 1975.

———. *There Is a Way Out.* Lakemont, GA: CSA, 1975.

Huxley, Aldous. *The Doors of Perception and Heaven and Hell.* New York: Harper, 1954.

I

Ingraham, E.V. *Wells of Abundance.* Marina del Rey, CA: DeVorss, 1938.

J

Jampolsky, Gerald G. *Love is Letting Go of Fear.* New York: Bantam, 1970.

———. *Teach Only Love.* New York: Bantam, 1983.

Jeffers, Susan. *A Fearbusting Workshop.* Audiotape. Santa Monica CA: Hay House, 1999.

John of the Cross. *Dark Night of the Soul.* Trowbridge, Wiltshire, UK: Redwood, 1583.

John-Roger and Peter McWilliams. *Life 101.* Los Angeles: Prelude, 1990.

———*You Can't Afford the Luxury of A Negative Thought.* Los Angeles: Prelude, 1988.

Johnson, Robert A. *He.* New York: Harper, 1989.

———. *Inner Work: Using Dreams and Active Imagination for Personal*

Growth. San Francisco: Harper, 1986.

———. *Owning Your Own Shadow*. San Francisco: Harper, 1991.

Jones, Alexander, ed. *The Jerusalem Bible, Readers Edition*. New York: Doubleday, 1966.

Joy, W. Brugh. *Avalanche: Heretical Reflections on the Dark and the Light*. New York: Ballantine, 1990.

Jung, Carl G. *Man and His Symbols*. New York: Doubleday, 1964.

———. *Memories, Dreams, Reflections*. New York: Vintage, 1965.

———. *The Portable Jung*. New York: Viking, 1971.

———. "The Development of Personality," *CW*, Vol. 17, paragraph 84, 1954.

K

Kapleau, Philip. *The Three Pillars of Zen*. New York: Harper, 1966.

———. *The Wheel of Life and Death: A Practical and Spiritual Guide*. New York: Doubleday, 1989.

Keen, Sam. *Hymns to an Unknown God*. New York: Bantam, 1994.

Keleman, Stanley. *Living Your Dying*. New York: Random, 1974.

Kelley, David E., creator. *Chicago Hope*. Television. Production companies: 20th Century Fox Television and David E. Kelley Productions, 1994-2000.

Kepler, Thomas S., compiled by. *The Evelyn Underhill Reader*. New York: Abingdon, 1962.

Keyes, Ken. *Handbook to Higher Consciousness*. Berkeley, CA: Living Love Center, 1972.

Khema, Ayya. *When the Iron Eagle Flies*. New York: Penguin. 1991.

Klane, Robert, director. *Weekend at Bernie's*. Feature film. Production companies: Artimm, D&A Partnership, TriStar Pictures, and Victor Drai Productions, 1993.

Klimo, John and Pamela Rae Heath. *Suicide: What Really Happens in the Afterlife?* Berkeley, CA: North Atlantic, 2006.

Koestler, Arthur. *The Roots of Coincidence*. New York: Vintage, 1972.

Kramer, Kay and Herbert Kramer. *Conversations at Midnight: Coming to Terms With Death and Dying.* New York: Avon, 1993.

Krishnamurti, Jiddu, about. (No author cited.) "Jiddu Krishnamurti Biography," no date cited. http://www.age-of-the-sage.org/theosophy/krishnamurti.html

Krishnamurti, Jiddu. "Lecture Given by J. Krishnamurti, in 1929, when He Dissolved the Order of the Star of the East." 1929. http://www.katinkahesselink.net/kr/star.htm

Kubler-Ross, Elisabeth. *Death: The Final Stage of Growth.* Englewood Cliffs. NJ: Prentice-Hall, 1975.

L

Labat, Elisabeth-Paule. *The Presence of God.* New York: Paulist, 1979.

Lambrecht, Jan and Raymond Collins, eds. *God and Human Suffering.* Louvain, Belgium: Peeters Press, 1990.

Langley, Noel. *Edgar Cayce on Reincarnation.* New York: Warner, 1967.

Lao-Tzu. *Tao Te Ching.* Foreword and Notes by Stephen Miller. New York: Harper, 1988.

Lauf, Detlef Ingo. *Secret Doctrines of the Tibetan Books of the Dead.* Boston: Shambhala, 1975.

Laut, Paul. *Money Is My Friend.* Cincinnati, OH: Trinity, 1978.

Leadbetter, C.W. *The Astral Plane.* Adyar Madras, India: Theosophical Publishing, 1895.

Lewis, C.S. *Mere Christianity.* New York: Collier, 1943.

Lhalungpa, Lobsang P. *The Life of Milarepa.* Boulder, CO: Shambhala, 1984.

Linklater, Richard, writer/director. *Waking Life.* Feature film. Production companies: Fox Searchlight Pictures, The Independent Film Channel, Thousand Words, Flat Black Films, Detour Filmproduction, and Line Research, 2001.

Lorr, Regina E and Robert W. Crary. *The Path of Light.* Marina Del Rey, CA: DeVorss, 1983.

Losang, Rato. *My Life and Lives: The Story of a Tibetan Incarnation.* New York: Dutton, 1977.

Lowen, Alexander. *The Spirituality of the Body: Bioenergetics for Grace and Harmony.* New York: Macmillan, 1990.

Lutyens, Mary. *Krishnamurti: The Years of Awakening.* New York: Farrar, Straus and Giroux, 1975.

M

Martin, James. *Suffering Man, Loving God.* San Francisco: Harper, 1990.

Matsunami, Kodo. *Introducing Buddhism.* Rutland, VT: Charles E Tuttle, 1965.

Maurer, Armand A, trans. *Master Eckhart: Parisian Questions and Prologues.* Toronto: Pontifical Institute of Mediaeval Studies, 1974.

May, Rollo. *The Courage to Create.* New York: Bantam, 1975.

———. *The Discovery of Being.* New York: Norton, 1983.

McDonald, Phoebe. *Dreams: Night Language of the Soul.* New York: Continuum, 1987.

Merton, Thomas. *Disputed Questions.* New York: Farrar, Straus and Giroux, 1953.

Metzner, Ralph. *Opening to Inner Life.* Los Angeles: Tarcher, 1986.

Miller, Alice. *Banished Knowledge.* New York: Doubleday, 1988.

———. *For Your Own Good: Hidden Cruelty in Child-Rearing and the Roots of Violence.* New York: Farrar Straus Giroux, 1980.

———. *The Drama of the Gifted Child* (formerly *Prisoners of Childhood*). New York: Basic, 1981.

———. *Thou Shalt Not Beware: Society's Betrayal of the Child.* New York: Meridian, 1981.

———. *The Untouched Key.* New York: Doubleday, 1988.

Ming-Dao, Deng. *365 Tao.* San Francisco: Harper, 1993.

———. *Chronicles of Tao.* San Francisco: Harper, 1993.

Mitford, Jessica. *The American Way of Death.* New York: Simon & Schuster, 1963.

Montagu, Ashley. *Touching.* New York: Harper, 1971.

Montana, Tony and Mark Brian Smith, directors. *Overnight.* Documentary. Production companies: Think Film and Black & White Pictures, 2003.

Montgomery, Ruth. *Companions Along the Way.* New York: Fawcett, 1974.

———. *Here and Hereafter.* New York: Random, 1968.

———. *The World Before.* New York: Fawcett, 1976.

———. *A World Beyond.* New York: Ballantine, 1971.

Moody, Raymond. A. *Life After Life.* New York: Bantam, 1975.

———. *Reflections on Life After Life.* Harrisburg. PA: Stackpole, 1977.

Moore, Thomas. *Care of the Soul.* New York: Harper, 1992.

Morgan, Campbell G. *The Analyzed Bible.* Westwood, NJ: Fleming H. Revell, 1964.

Morse, Melvin. *Closer to the Light.* New York: Villard, 1990.

———. *Transformed by the Light.* New York: Villard, 1992.

Myer, Muffie, director. *The New Medicine.* Documentary. Production companies: Gorton Studios and Twin Cities Public Television, 2006.

Myss, Caroline. *Anatomy of the Spirit.* New York: Three Rivers, 1997.

———. *Caroline Myss: The Energetics of Healing.* DVD. Production company: Wellspring, 1999.

———. *Sacred Contracts: Awakening Your Divine Potential* New York: Three Rivers, 2003.

———. *Why People Don't Heal and How They Can.* New York: Three Rivers, 1998.

———. *Why People Don't Heal / Three Levels of Power.* DVD. Production company: Wellspring, 2004.

———. See also http://www.myss.com for a complete list of DVDs, books, and a calendar of events.

N

Nelson, Ruby. *The Door of Everything.* Marina del Rey, CA: DeVorss, 1963.

Neu, Eva Renee. *Dreams and Dream Groups: Messages From the Interior.* Freedom, CA: Crossing, 1988.

Neufeldt, Ronald W, ed. *Karma and Rebirth: Post Classical Development.* Albany. NY: State University of New York Press, 1986.

Nicoll, Maurice. *Living Time.* Boulder, CO: Shambhala, 1984.

Northrup, Christiane. *The Wisdom of Menopause.* New York: Bantam, 2006.

———. *Women's Bodies, Women's Wisdom.* New York: Bantam, 1998.

Norwood, Robin. *Why Me? Why This? Why Now?* New York: Carol Southern, 1994.

Novak, Philip. *The World's Wisdom: Sacred Texts of the World's Religions.* San Francisco: Harper, 1994.

O

Ornstein, Robert E. *The Mind Field.* New York: Viking, 1976.

Osis, Karlis and Erlundur Haraldsson. *At the Hour of Death.* New York: Hastings, 1977.

Ouspensky, P.D. *In Search of the Miraculous.* Orlando, FL: Harcourt, 1949.

———. *The Psychology of Man's Possible Evolution.* New York: Vintage, 1950.

P

Parker, DeWitt H., ed. *Schopenhauer Selections.* New York: Charles Scribner's Sons, 1928.

Pearce, Joseph Chlton. *The Crack in the Cosmic Egg.* New York: Simon & Schuster, 1973.

Peale, Norman Vincent. *The Power of Positive Thinking.* Pawling NY: Peale Center for Christian Living, 1978.

Peat, F. David. *Synchronicity: The Bridge Between Matter and Mind.* New York: Bantam, 1987.

Peck, M. Scott. *The Road Less Traveled.* New York: Simon & Schuster, 1978.

———. *A World Waiting to be Born.* New York: Bantam, 1993.

Phillips, Michael. *The Seven Laws of Money.* New York: Random, 1974.

Pierrakos, Eva. *The Pathwork of Self-Transformation.* New York: Bantam, 1990.

Pinsky, Drew. *Anderson Cooper 360.* CNN. Airdate: August 27, 2007.

Pipitone, Phyllis L. *The Inner World of Dreams.* Bryn Mawr, PA: Dorrance, 1987.

Ponce, Charles. *Working the Soul..* Berkeley, CA: North Atlantic, 1988.

Ponder, Catherine. *Open Your Mind to Prosperity.* Marina del Rey, CA: De Vorss, 1971.

Porter, David. *Mother Teresa: The Early Years.* Grand Rapids, MI: William B. Eerdmans, 1986.

Price, William Randolph. *The Superbeings.* New York: Ballantine, 1975.

PR Newswire (no author cited). "Carolyn K. Reidy Named President and Chief Executive Officer of Simon & Schuster, Inc.," CNNMoney.com, September 6, 2007. http://money.cnn.com/news/newsfeeds/articles/prnewswire/NYTH0300609 2007-1.htm

Project for Excellence in Journalism, The. "Ownership." *The State of the News Media 2006*, 2006. http://www.stateofthenewsmedia.org/2006/narrative_networktv_ownership.asp?cat=5&media=5

R

Rahner, Karl. *Theological Investigations, Vol. XIX.* New York: Crossroad, 1983.

Raffia, Swami. *Living With the Himalayan Masters.* Honesdale, PA: Himalayan Institute, 1978.

Rapaille, Clotaire. *The Culture Code.* New York: Broadway, 2007.

Ray, James. List of speaking engagements. http://jamesray.com/events/creating-wealth-experience.php

Reed, Henry. *Edgar Cayce on Mysteries of the Mind*. New York: Warner, 1989.

Reeve, Christopher. *Still Me*. New York: Ballantine, 1999.

Reid, Clyde H. *Dreams: Discovering Your Inner Teacher*. Minneapolis, MN: Winston, 1983.

Religious Tolerance (no author cited). *Religious Beliefs of Americans*, 2003. http://www.religioustolerance.org/chr_poll3.htm

Reps, Paul, compiled by. *Zen Flesh, Zen Bones*. New York: Doubleday, 1994.

Ressner, Jeffrey. "The Secret of Success," *Time*, December 26, 2006. http://www.time.com/time/arts/article/0,8599,1573136,00.html

Rice, Richard. *God's Foreknowledge and Man's Free Will*. Minneapolis, MN: Bethany, 1980.

Richard, Lucien. *What Are They Saying About the Theology of Suffering*? New York: Paulist, 1992.

Rinpoche, Sogyal. *The Tibetan Book of Living and Dying*. San Francisco: Harper, 1992.

Ring. Kenneth. *Heading Toward Omega*. New York: Morrow, 1984.

———. *Life at Death*. New York: Coward, McCann & Geoghegan, 1980.

Roberts, Jane. *Dreams, "Evolution," and Value Fulfillment, Vol. II*. New York: Prentice-Hall, 1986.

———. *The Nature of Personal Reality: A Seth Book*. New York: Prentice-Hall, 1974.

———. *The Nature of the Psyche, Its Human Expression: A Seth Book*. New York: Prentice-Hall, 1979.

———. *The Seth Material*. New York: Prentice-Hall, 1970.

———. *Seth Speaks: The Eternal Validity of the Soul*. New York: Prentice-Hall, 1972.

———. *The "Unknown" Reality: A Seth Book, Vol. I*. New York: Prentice-Hall, 1977.

———. *The "Unknown" Reality: A Seth Book, Vol. II.* New York: Prentice-Hall, 1979.

———. *The Individual and the Nature of Mass Events: A Seth Book.* New York: Prentice-Hall, 1981.

Rogness, Michael. *The Hand That Holds Me.* Minneapolis, MN: Augsberg, 1984.

Ross, Ruth. *Prospering Woman.* Mill Valley, CA: Whatever, 1982.

S

Saraydarian, Torkom. *The Spring of Prosperity.* Agoura, CA: Aquarian Educational Group, 1982.

Schickel, Richard. director *Spielberg on Spielberg.* Documentary. Production company: TMC, 2007.

Schiller, David. *The Little Zen Companion.* New York: Workman, 1994.

Scorsese, Martin, director. *Goodfellas.* Feature Film. Production company: Warner, 1990.

Shilling, Paul. *God and Human Anguish.* Nashville, TN: Abingdon, 1977.

Schucman, Helen and William Thetford. *A Course in Miracles.* Tiburon, CA: Foundation for Inner Peace, 1975.

Schumacher, E.F. *A Guide for the Perplexed.* New York: Harper, 1977.

Schweitzer, Albert. *The Words of Albert Schweitzer Selected by Norman Cousins.* New York: Newmarket, 1984.

Senzaki, Nyogen and Ruth Strout McCandless, compiled by. *Buddhism and Zen.* New York: The Wisdom Library. 1953.

Sheehy, Gail. *Pathfinders.* New York: Morrow, 1981.

———. *Love Medicine & Miracles.* New York: Harper, 1986.

Short, Susanne. "Whispering of the Walls." In *Reclaiming the Inner Child,* edited by Jeremiah Abrams. Los Angeles: Tarcher, 1990, 198-203. See also pp. 33-38 at http://www.personaltransformation.com/PDFs/Issue2.pdf

Siegel, Bernie S. *Peace Love and Healing.* New York: Harper, 1989.
Simonton, Carl, Stephanie Matthews-Simonton, and James L Creighton. *Getting Well Again.* New York: Bantam, 1978.
Simonton, O. Carl and Reid Henson. *The Healing Journey.* New York: Bantam, 1992.
Sinetar, Marsha. *Do What You Love, The Money Will Follow.* New York: Paulist, 1987.
Singer, June. *Boundaries of the Soul.* New York: Doubleday, 1972.
Singh, Tara. *Love Holds No Grievances.* Los Angeles: Life Action, 1988.
Sinkler, Lorraine. *The Spiritual Journey of Joel S. Goldsmith.* New York: Harper, 1973.
Skutch, Robert. *Journey Without Distance: The Story Behind A Course in Miracles.* Berkeley, CA: Celestial Arts, 1984.
Smith, Huston. *The Religions of Man.* New York: Harper, 1958.
Soelle, Dorothee. *Suffering.* Minneapolis, MN: Fortress Press, 1975.
Sparrow, Lynn Elwell. *Reincarnation: Claiming Your Past, Creating Your Future.* New York: Harper, 1988.
Speller, Jon P. *Seed Money in Action: Working the Law of Tenfold Return.* New York: Robert Speller & Sons, 1965.
Spretnak, Charlene. *States of Grace.* New York: Harper, 1991.
Stark, Harold Richter. *A Doctor Goes to Heaven.* Boerne, TX: Quartus, 1982.
Stearn, Jess. *Edgar Cayce -The Sleeping Prophet.* New York: Bantam, 1967.
———. *Soul Mates.* New York: Bantam, 1967.
Steiner, Rudolf. *The Principle of Spiritual Economy.* Hudson, NY: Anthroposophic Press, 1909.
Stuart, David. *Alan Watts.* Briarcliff Manor, NY: Stein and Day, 1976.
Styron, William. *Darkness Visible.* New York: Random, 1990.
Sugrue, Thomas. *There is a River: The Story of Edgar Cayce.* Virginia Beach VA: A.R.E. Press, 1942.
Suzuki, D.T. *An Introduction to Zen Buddhism.* New York: Grove,

1934.

Swedenborg, Emanuel. *Heaven and Hell.* New York: Swedenborg Foundation, 1758.

Szasz, Thomas. *The Myth of Psychotherapy.* Garden City, NY: Doubleday, 1978.

T

Taylor, Humphrey. *The Religious and Other Beliefs of Americans 2003,* 2004. http://www.harrisinteractive.com/harris_poll/index.asp?PID=359. See also Harris Interactive (no author cited). *The Religious and Other Beliefs of Americans 2005,* 2006. http://www.harrisinteractive.com/harris_poll/ index.asp?PID=618

Teilhard de Chardin, Pierre. *On Suffering.* New York: Harper, 1974.

Thomson, Sandra, A. *Cloud Nine: A Dreamer's Dictionary.* New York: Avon, 1994.

Thurman, Robert. *Robert Thurman on Buddhism.* DVD. Production company: Wellspring, 2002.

Thurston, Mark. *Discovering Your Soul's Purpose.* Virginia Beach, VA: A.R.E. Press, 1984.

Toms, Michael. *At the Leading Edge.* Burdett, NY: Larson, 1991.

Todeschi, Kevin J. *Edgar Cayce on the Akashic Records.* Virginia Beach, VA: A.R.E. Press, 1998. Edgar Cayce Readings © 1971, 1999-2005 by the Edgar Cayce Foundation. Used by permission. All Rights Reserved. http://www.edgarcayce.org/about_ec/cayce_on/akashic/

Troward, Thomas. *The Dore Lectures.* New York: Dodd Mead, 1909.

———. *The Edinburgh Lectures on Mental Science.* New York: Dodd Mead, 1909.

Trungpa, Chogyam. *Orderly Chaos: The Mandala Principle.* Boston: Shambhala, 1991.

———. *Shambhala: The Sacred Path of the Warrior.* Boston: Shambhala, 1984.

———. *Transcending Madness: The Experience of the Six Bardos.* Boston:

Shambhala, 1992.

U

Underhill, Evelyn. The Spiritual Life. New York: Harper, 1936. See also http://www.mrrena.com/misc/sl.shtml

V

Vaughan, Frances and Roger Walsh, eds. *A Gift of Peace: Selections From A Course in Miracles.* Los Angeles: Tarcher, 1986.

Von Franz, Marie-Louise. *On Dreams and Death.* Boston: Shambhala, 1986.

Vranich, Belisa. *Anderson Cooper 360.* CNN. Airdate: August 27, 2007.

W

Warnaco, Kenneth. *A Talk Given on a Course in Miracles: An Introduction.* Roscoe, NY: Foundation for "A Course in Miracles," 1983.

Watts, Alan W. *The Meaning of Happiness.* New York: Harper, 1940.

———. *The Wisdom of Insecurity,* New York: Vintage, 1951.

———. *Does it Matter?* New York: Random, 1968.

Weber, Renee. *Dialogues With Scientists and Sages.* New York: Routledge & Kegan Paul, 1986.

Weiss, Jess, E. *The Vestibule,* Port Washington, NY: Ashley, 1972.

Welch, John. *Spiritual Pilgrims.* New York: Paulist, 1982.

Wheelis, Allen. *How People Change,* New York: Harper, 1969.

White, John, ed. *What is Enlightenment?* Los Angeles: Tarcher, 1984.

Whitmont, Edward C. *Return of the Goddess.* New York: Crossroad, 1982.

———. *The Symbolic Quest,* New York, CG Jung Foundation, 1969.

Whitney, Barry L. *What Are They Saying About God and Evil?* New York: Paulist, 1989.

Wiesel, Elie. *The Night Trilogy.* New York: Farrar, Straus & Giroux, 1972.

Wikipedia. No author cited. "Chemical Imbalances in Clinical Depression," no date cited. http://en.wikipedia.org/wiki/Chemical_imbalance_theory#Clinical_depression

———. No author cited. "Alternative Medicine," no date cited. http://en.wikipedia.org/wiki/Alternative_medicine

———. No author cited. "Carl Jung," no date cited. http://en.wikipedia.org/wiki/Carl_Jung

———. No author cited. "Alice Miller," no date cited. http://en.wikipedia.org/wiki/Alice_Miller_%28psychologist%29

Wilber, Ken. *Eye to Eye: The Quest for the New Paradigm*. New York: Doubleday, 1983.

Wilde, Stuart. *Miracles,* Taos, NM: White Dove, 1983.

Williamson, Marianne. *Illuminata*. New York: Random, 1994.

———. *A Return to Love*. New York: Harper, 1992.

Wilson, Colin. *Afterlife*. New York: Doubleday, 1987.

———. *CG Jung, Lord of the Underworld*. New York: Sterling, 1984.

Wilson, Ian. *The After Death Experience: The Physics of the Non- Physical*. New York: Morrow, 1987.

Wise County Messenger (no author cited). "Kim Tinkham Believes She Can Cure her Breast Cancer Herself," April 1, 2007. http://www.wcmessenger.com/news/news/EEZVuVFyFZvtdbUrLt.php

Wolfe, George C., director. *Lackawanna Blues*. Feature film. Production companies: HBO Films and HBO Pictures, 2005.

Woodward, Mary Anne. *Edgar Cayce's Story of Karma*. New York: Berkley, 1971.

———. *Scars of the Soul*. Columbus, OH: Brindabella, 1985.

Y

Yogananda, Paramahansa. *Autobiography of a Yogi*. Los Angeles: Self-Realization Fellowship, 1946.

———. *Man's Eternal Quest*. Los Angeles: Self-Realization Fellowship, 1975.

Z

Zacharias, Paul. *Insights Into the Beyond.* New York: Swedenborg, 1976.

Zukav, Gary. *The Seat of the Soul.* New York: Simon & Schuster, 1989.

Zweig, Connie and Jeremiah Abrams, eds. *Meeting the Shadow.* Los Angeles: Tarcher, 1991.

Zweig, Stefan. *Mental Healers.* New York: Viking, 1932.

Articles

Adler, Jerry. "Decoding the Secret," *Newsweek*, March 5, 2007. http://www.msnbc.msn.com/id/17314883/site/newsweek/

Age of the Sage (no author cited). "Jiddu Krishnamurti Biography." No date cited. http://www.age-of-the-sage.org/theosophy/krishnamurti.html

Bhushan, Ranjit. "Osama Bin Laden: CIA's Toy Gone Awry." *Outlook* . New Delhi, India, Sept. 17, 2001. In *World Press Review*, Vol. 48, #11. http://www.worldpress.org/1101binladen_cia.htm

Duncan, David Ewing. "The Pollution Within," *National Geographic*, October 2006. http://www3.nationalgeographic.com/ngm/0610/feature4/index.html and http://www.davidewingduncan.net/about_david.htm

Forbes Magazine (no author cited). "Forbes 100 List," *Forbes.* http://www.forbes.com/lists/2007/53/07celebrities_Rhonda-Byrne_JYV0.html

Holland, Jimmie. "The Tyranny of Positive Thinking," adapted from the book, *The Human Side of Cancer, Living with Hope, Coping with Uncertainty*, by Jimmie Holland and Sheldon Lewis. New York: Harper, 2001. See also http://www.humansideofcancer.com/chapter2/chapter.2.htm and http://www.leukemia-lymphoma.org/all_page?item_id=7038

Jung, Carl. "The Development of Personality," *CW,* Vol. 17, paragraph 84, 1954.

Krishnamurti, Jiddu. (no author cited.)"Jiddu Krishnamurti Biography." (no date cited.) http://www.age-of-the-sage.org/theosophy/krishnamurti.html

Krishnamurti, Jiddu. "Lecture Given by J. Krishnamurti, in 1929, When He Dissolved the Order of the Star of the East." 1929. http://www.katinkahesselink.net/kr/star.htm

PR Newswire (no author cited). "Carolyn K. Reidy Named President and Chief Executive Officer of Simon & Schuster, Inc.," CNNMoney.com, September 6, 2007. http://money.cnn.com/news/newsfeeds/articles/prnewswire/NYTH03006092007-1.htm

Ressner, Jeffrey. "The Secret of Success," *Time*, December 26, 2006. http://www.time.com/time/arts/article/0,8599,1573136,00.html

Short, Susanne. "Whispering of the Walls." In *Reclaiming the Inner Child,* edited by Jeremiah Abrams. Los Angeles: Tarcher, 1990, 198-203. See also pp 33-38 at http://www.personaltransformation.com/PDFs/Issue2.pdf

Todeschi, Kevin J.. *Edgar Cayce on the Akashic Records.* Virginia Beach, VA: A.R.E. Press, 1998. http://www.edgarcayce.org/about_ec/cayce_on/akashic/

Wikipedia. No author cited. "Chemical Imbalances in Clinical Depression," no date cited. http://en.wikipedia.org/wiki/Chemical_imbalance_theory#Clinical_depression

———. No author cited. "Alternative Medicine," no date cited. http://en.wikipedia.org/wiki/Alternative_medicine

———. No author cited. "Carl Jung," no date cited. http://en.wikipedia.org/wiki/Carl_Jung

———. No author cited. "Alice Miller," no date cited. http://en.wikipedia.org/wiki/Alice_Miller_%28psychologist%29

Wise County Messenger (no author cited). "Kim Tinkham Believes She Can Cure her Breast Cancer Herself," April 1, 2007. http://www.wcmessenger.com/news/news/EEZVuVFyFZvtdbUrLt.php

Online References

Adler, Jerry. "Decoding the Secret," *Newsweek*, March 5, 2007. http://www.msnbc.msn.com/id/17314883/site/newsweek

Age of the Sage (no author cited). *Jiddu Krishnamurti Biography* http://www.age-of-the-sage.org/theosophy/krishnamurti.html

Duncan, David Ewing. "The Pollution Within," *National Geographic*, October 2006. http://www3.nationalgeographic.com/ngm/0610/feature4/index.html and http://www.davidewingduncan.net/about_david.htm

Forbes Magazine (no author cited). "Forbes 100 List," *Forbes.* http://www.forbes.com/lists/2007/53/07celebrities_Rhonda-Byrne_JYV0.html

Harris Interactive (no author cited). *The Religious and Other Beliefs of Americans 2005*, 2006. http://www.harrisinteractive.com/harris_poll/index.asp?PID=618. See also: Taylor, Humphrey. *The Religious and Other Beliefs of Americans 2003*, 2004. http://www.harrisinteractive.com/harris_poll/index.asp?PID=359.

Holland, Jimmie. "The Tyranny of Positive Thinking," adapted from the book, *The Human Side of Cancer, Living with Hope, Coping with Uncertainty*, by Jimmie Holland and Sheldon Lewis. New York: Harper, 2001. See also http://www.humansideofcancer.com/chapter2/chapter.2.htm and http://www.leukemia-lymphoma.org/all_page?item_id=7038

Krishnamurti, Jiddu, about (no author cited). *Jiddu Krishnamurti Biography.* http://www.age-of-the-sage.org/theosophy/krishnamurti.html

Krishnamurti, Jiddu. *Lecture Given by J. Krishnamurti, in* 1929, *When He Dissolved the Order of the Star of the East.* Copyright 1998 — KFA; All Rights Reserved, Krishnamurti Foundation of America. http://www.katinkahesselink.net/kr/star.htm

Myss, Caroline. List of books, DVDs, tapes, and calendar of events: http://www.myss.com

Ray, James. List of speaking engagements. http://jamesray.com/events/creating-wealth-experience.php

ReligiousTolerance.org (no author cited). *Religious Beliefs of Americans*, 2003. http://www.religioustolerance.org/chr_poll3.htm

Ressner, Jeffrey. "The Secret of Success," *Time*, December 26, 2006. http://www.time.com/time/arts/article/0,8599,1573136,00.html

Short, Susanne. *Whispering of the Walls.* http://www.personaltransformation.com/PDFs/Issue2.pdf. 33-38.

Taylor, Humphrey. *The Religious and Other Beliefs of Americans 2003*, 2004. http://www.harrisinteractive.com/harris_poll/index.asp?PID=359. See also Harris Interactive (no author cited). *The Religious and Other Beliefs of Americans 2005*, 2006. http://www.harrisinteractive.com/harris_poll/index.asp?PID=618

Todeschi, Kevin J.. *Edgar Cayce on the Akashic Records.* Virginia Beach, VA:

A.R.E. Press, 1998. http://www.edgarcayce.org/about_ec/cayce_on/akashic/

Underhill, Evelyn. *The Spiritual Life.* See also http://www.mrrena.com/misc/sl.shtml, 1936.

Wikipedia (no author cited). "Chemical Imbalances in Clinical Depression." http://en.wikipedia.org/wiki/Chemical_imbalance_theory# Clinical_depression, no date cited.

———. (no author cited). "Alternative Medicine," no date cited. http://en.wikipedia.org/wiki/Alternative_medicine

——— (no author cited). "Carl Jung." http://en.wikipedia.org/wiki/Carl_Jung, no date cited.

——— (no author cited). "Alice Miller." http://en.wikipedia.org/wiki/Alice_Miller_%28psychologist%29, no date cited.

World Press (no author cited). *Osama Bin Laden: CIA's Toy Gone Awry*, September 17, 2001. http://www.worldpress.org/1101binladen_cia.htm

Films

Features

DeNiro, Robert, director. *A Bronx Tale.* Production companies: B.T. Films, Penta Entertainment, Price Entertainment, and Tribeca Productions, 1993.

Haas, Philip, director. *The Music of Chance.* Production companies: I.R.S. and Transatlantic Release, 1993.

Klane, Robert, director. *Weekend at Bernie's.* Production companies: Artimm, D&A Partnership, TriStar Pictures, and Victor Drai Productions, 1993.

Linklater, Richard, writer/director. *Waking Life.* Production companies: Fox Searchlight Pictures, The Independent Film Channel, Thousand Words,

Flat Black Films, Detour Filmproduction, and Line Research, 2001.

Scorsese, Martin, director. *Goodfellas*. Production company: Warner Bros, 1990.

Wolfe, George C., director. *Lackawanna Blues*. Production companies: HBO Films and HBO Pictures, 2005.

Documentaries

Montana, Tony and Mark Brian Smith, directors. *Overnight*. Production companies: Think Film and Black & White Pictures, 2003.

Myer, Muffie, director. *The New Medicine*. Production companies: Gorton Studios and Twin Cities Public Television, 2006.

Schickel, Richard, director. *Spielberg on Spielberg*,. Production company: TMC, 2007.

DVDs

Lectures

Myss, Caroline. *Caroline Myss: The Energetics of Healing*. Production company: Wellspring, 1999.

———. *Why People Don't Heal/Three Levels of Power*. Production company: Wellspring, 2004.

Thurman, Robert. *Robert Thurman on Buddhism*. Production company: Wellspring, 2002.

Other

Heriot, Drew. *The Secret*. Production companies: Prime Time Productions, Nine Network Australia, and T.S. Production, 2006.

TV Shows

About *The Secret*

The Ellen DeGeneres Show. Syndicated. Airdate: December 1, 2006.

Larry King Live. CNN. Airdates: November 16, 2006 and March 8, 2007.

The Oprah Winfrey Show. Syndicated. Airdates: February 8, 2007, March 5, 2007, and March 26, 2007.

About "Acquired Narcissism"

Anderson Cooper 360. CNN. Airdate: August 27, 2007, with Dr. Drew Pinsky and Belisa Vranich.

Episodic

Carter, Thomas, Fred Gerber and Bobby Roth, directors. *Hack.* Production companies: Big Ticket Productions and CBS Television, 2002-2004.

Kelley, David E., creator. *Chicago Hope.* Production companies: 20th Century Fox Television and David E. Kelley Productions, 1994-2000.

Misc

Game Plan greeting card, serial number B-259275. Date and place unknown.

Jeffers, Susan. *A Fearbusting Workshop.* Audiotape. Santa Monica CA: Hay House, 1999.

Index

T

About the Author

Born in Toronto and raised in Montreal, Carol Rutter graduated with a Bachelor of Fine Arts degree from Concordia University in 1988, two years before she won the Green Card lottery and moved to Los Angeles. She now resides in Florida and can be reached at NewAgeJunkie1 at Yahoo.com.

Carol's 100+ published articles have appeared in *Film Comment, The San Francisco Examiner, Astronomy, Cinema Canada, Splash*, and others.